THE YEARS OF SMASHING BRICKS

AN ANECDOTAL MEMOIR

Books by Richard Katrovas

Poetry
Green Dragons
Snug Harbor
The Public Mirror
The Book of Complaints
Dithyrambs
Prague Winter

Prose
Prague, USA
The Republic of Burma Shave
Mystic Pig: A Novel of New Orleans
The Years of Smashing Bricks

The Years of Smashing Bricks

An anecdotal memoir

Richard Katrovas

Carnegie Mellon University Press
Pittsburgh 2007

Library of Congress Control Number: 200622932
ISBN- 13: 978-0-88748-465-0
ISBN- 10: 0-88748-468-9
Copyright © 2007 by Richard Katrovas
Printed and bound in the United States of America

10 9 8 7 6 5 4 3 2 1

Contents

1967–69

Karate is as much a collection of anecdotes as a preparation for body-to-body combat. The aspect of it that isn't a minor, goofy sport is closer to ballet or opera than to self-defense. When I studied karate in Sasebo, Japan at fourteen, fifteen and sixteen, *Madame Butterfly* played endlessly in the baroque theater of my adolescent groin. It was the old story, the oldest story, of urges conflicting with prohibitions. When I performed the karate dances, the kata, I expressed the urge for nobility coalescing in my own roiling chemistry.

I lived in Sasebo from 1967 to the end of 1969. My brother and I had been adopted just months before we'd arrived. Our new parents had three children of their own, so our family was composed of a naval lieutenant who'd climbed into officer rank from noncom, a naval wife who was our real father's sister, and their two daughters and toddler son. We were an odd, bifurcated American family the two parts of which didn't know the other. The father spent most of our three years in Sasebo sweeping mines off the coast of Vietnam, and the mother was overwhelmed, by turns frantic and forlorn. She feared for her husband, was unhappy abroad, and angry that she'd adopted my brother and me a few months earlier. She was thirty-one.

Sasebo is the southernmost port city on the southern island of Kyushu. It's close enough to Nagasaki that one should wonder if any fallout had rained down upon it, though no one ever did so wonder, at least not aloud. The parts of downtown Sasebo I saw, was able to see, were geared for Navy business: hundreds of sleaze pits, bars seething with hookers, just outside the base, north across a brief stone bridge, within blocks of Dragon Heights, where flag rank's privileged broods nested in sprawling bungalows.

A tall child, I looked a few years older than my age. Sex was a heaven I could only imagine, and I spent all of my hours, waking and sleeping, doing so.

I stole a modest sum from my stepmother and paid a hooker for sex. Then another and another and another. My stepmother eventually missed the money; I confessed to the thefts but not to the purchases they enabled. I was frightened of my stepmother because she was angry all the time and clearly didn't like me. I didn't like her, either, and felt guilty that I didn't. I was six feet tall, skinny, with a crew cut. I had zits all around my big lips, big nose, big eyes. I looked like a sailor, a gooney baby sailor, a seaman second class everybody was obliged to shit upon, but who got to go out, every few months when his ship was in port, and buy sex. I was three years younger than the youngest sailors when I confessed to stealing money from my stepmother's underwear drawer. I was scared of being a coward, ashamed of my desires, and spent most of my time, out of school, practicing karate at the Special Services gym on the base.

I was good at the dances, the kata, and I was pretty good at the full-contact sparring with pads, and I was quite good at breaking things with my hands. The sparring and breaking had practical application: by virtue of my training, I was probably better able to deal with physical confrontations than I otherwise would have been, but that may not be saying much in the grand scheme of male aggression. The kata, I realized only years later, after I'd taught karate for part of my meager living for several years, have little to do with preparing one for combat with other men. They are about the inner battle, the need to express dignity in a world bent upon wresting it away.

The horror of my crimes, of stealing money from the woman who'd saved my life; of using that money to buy sex; of masturbating at the drop of a hat, a coin, a shoe, the sun; of disliking the woman I'd called mother for less than a year, the same length of time I'd known her minus a couple of months; of leaving my dying real mother and three younger siblings, allowing my criminal father to flee with my brother and me west to his sister in California; of being the son of a criminal, a man who'd spent half of my childhood in prison, the other half kiting checks across the entire United States, except Alaska; of not understanding what the war in Vietnam was for, but most of all for being a coward; the horror of all these crimes melted away when I danced those stories of noble confrontation, when my body would become something ageless and ancient, moving through geometric patterns older than the issues of the day and all their antecedents. The kata were the peaceful place of my odd and turbulent youth, the only solace, other than sex, to my clumsy life, though unlike sex they centered on a truth beyond gratification. They were the foil of my clownish lust, the compass pointing always toward the true and tragic nature of existence, even as in coming years I staggered mindlessly, giddily, from woman to woman to woman.

By the time we left Sasebo, most of my zits had faded. I'd spent my early teens in a beautiful, strange city, learned enough Japanese to get around the dojo, which wasn't much. In Coronado, I became the weird guy no one messed with because he "knew karate"; it was a time when the mystique of the black belt was at its height, before Tai Kwan Do became a cottage industry churning out thousands of dubious black belts. I sang in the high school choir and wrote and read poetry and novels, earned mediocre grades. I taught karate and worked twenty hours a week in a cafeteria on the Amphibious Base. I entered the seventies wide-eyed, and perhaps a little more emotionally disoriented than most other teens. Coronado Island was the home of my youth, my true point of departure, the center of the dance.

Roughly ten percent of this book is fabrication; I've changed a few names and sometimes dovetailed two or three individuals into one. I've tried not to embellish too much, though I've probably failed miserably at restraining a natural inclination to render the world, if not my life, more intriguing than it is.

We condescend to our former selves at our peril, and I've attempted here to treat my younger self with compassion, even though my stronger inclination is to reach back in time and smack him hard on the back of his head. He was a fool, but desired mightily not to be, and I give him some credit for that.

The Year of Smashing Bricks

Spring, 1973

I was 6′1″, skinny, androgynously pretty with thick long dark hair. I was a mediocre athlete but had a talent for hitting things with my hands. I'd received a second-degree black belt in Sho-bu-kan Okinawa-te, in Sasebo, Japan, where my uncle/stepfather, a low-ranking naval officer, had been stationed for almost three years before getting sent back to San Diego, California. I'd gotten the black belt primarily because I was good at teaching kata to the sailors who came and went, and because I was pretty good at freestyle sparring and real good at smashing stacks of Japanese roof tiles. Upon returning at the very end of 1969, we lived on Coronado, which isn't an island; seven miles of artificial Silver Strand make it, technically, a peninsula, but since Imperial Beach, a suburb of Tijuana that just happens to be on the U.S. side of the border, lay at the other end of the Strand, Coronado was, in all its xenophobic, militaristic glory, an island.

Hemmed on its north and south by huge U.S. Navy bases, North Island Naval Air Station and the Amphibious Base, Coronado was a bedroom community of palm-lined streets and manicured lawns; its heart was the Hotel Del Coronado, where *Some Like It Hot* had been filmed, and whose Victorian, sprawling beachfront I loved to cruise on acid. In 1972, I first dropped acid and first voted—Orange Barrel Sunshine and for McGovern, though not simultaneously, as I recall—and sat with my buddies, all of whom had been born in 1953, to hear our draft lottery numbers announced over the radio. Mine was 339, a winner. I knew I wouldn't get drafted unless the entire nation of China set out paddling for the West Coast.

I was of course terrified of going to war, and couldn't believe the preternatural grind guys my age were subjecting themselves to for the privilege of getting onto the UDT and the SEAL team, hustling double-time for miles along the waterline in heavy black boots behind the Hotel Del Coronado (the "Del"), from the Amphibious base to the fence of North Island, chanting those creepy rhymes.

I'd sit in the "Captain's Chair," as Barney Ward dubbed it, an outcropping of granite in the rough shape of a throne that overlooked the ocean behind the Del, and watch them trot in syncopation along the shore. Their heads were shaved. They wore tee-shirts and long olive pants and their spit-shined black boots sank into the wet sand, making each stride literally suck. I'd smoke a joint and watch them, twenty or thirty, recede toward the North Island fence, then grow larger as they approached and passed. I'd smoke another joint and shake my head in wonder as they sucked sucked sucked out yet another mile.

One heard stories about them, that the Underwater Demolition Teams were composed of certifiable killers, that one simply did not fuck with them. They were like Marines but smarter and better, certainly meaner. And the guys who made it into the SEALS were transported to another zone of reality in which killing was an art, truly, in which "Martial Art" had resonance, and in which each of them was a meat machine fashioned for the purpose of stealthy murder.

I could smash a cinder block (sometimes), certain kinds of bricks (that hadn't been fired), and many kinds of rocks, with my hand, and would get drunk at keg parties and exhibit that skill whenever requested to do so. I could beat the hell out of a Makiwara board with my callused fists; indeed, I'd fight just about anybody anytime, and was very lucky I didn't get my skinny karate ass seriously mangled in 1972. But I escaped Vietnam by a roll of the bureaucratic dice (at least that's what I thought; it's doubtful that many draftees were being sent over in 1972), and a serious ass whipping by the sheerest dumb luck.

I met Louanna early that autumn. I'd quit Coronado High School in the fall of 1971, gone to L.A. to make my fortune as a songwriter and failed miserably and immediately. I'd whimpered back across that blue, arcing bridge to Coronado in early 1972, signed up for yoga and folk guitar in night school, and attended perhaps two sessions of each class; they gave me my diploma anyway. I enrolled at San Diego City College in the fall, and met Louanna there.

I was no virgin, except perhaps spiritually. But, with the exception of hookers in Sasebo, I'd never had sex with a real woman, that is, a grown-up female full of sadness and resolve, who had shed all girlish fears of physical intimacy. Louanna was long and gorgeous, and so feminine males ached in her presence. Cameron Crowe, my classmate in Greek Mythology that fall (he'd just finished living the *Almost Famous* part of his life) and someone I hung out with on campus, used to grin and call me a swine, his way of complimenting me for having daily (sometimes hourly) sex with so beautiful a female.

She was nuts and tried to kill herself twice in the bathroom, once with a razor once with pills, but that's another story, one that has to do with her father, a Bible-thumping prig who sent her hellfire letters that made her weep convulsively for hours; one, I suppose, that also has to do with the fact that she was recently divorced from a man who'd been a Marine in Vietnam, and who had spent much of his time there smack dab in the middle of the proverbial shit.

I, too, was insane. That is, I was a slave to desire; I went wherever it told me to, and that meant nightly, daily, hourly, into Louanna's arms. I could not stand it when she spoke on the phone to "Mikey," her ex-husband. I heard an intimacy in her voice that evaporated when she, always teary, hung up. Always when she got off the phone (of course I was too much of a child to give her privacy), I'd go out to the side of our little cottage in Coronado, a charming pink stucco structure behind a large house on Orange Avenue; it'd probably been servants' quarters in the Thirties and Forties. I'd go out and smash bricks with my right hand. I'd stack three bricks beside three bricks, set the edge of a brick on each pile, and then smack the hell out of it until it shattered. Then I'd do another. I got my bricks from a pile in the alley that seemed magically never to diminish.

I was nineteen; Louanna was several years older. She wanted to have sex all the time. All the time. Because I was nineteen, I could, at least for part of a year, accommodate her. I didn't understand that Louanna was with me primarily because I could have sex (almost) all the time, and because otherwise she didn't have to deal with me, that is, emotionally, because, of course, she still loved her ex-husband, who was unable to have sex with her at all.

At first I'd been happy to know that the reason Louanna had left "Mikey" was that he couldn't get the war out of his head. His head full of the horrors of war, he couldn't achieve erection, so in the beginning I didn't feel at all threatened by Louanna's ex-husband.

But as I'd smash bricks on the side of the pink cottage, I'd hear Louanna sobbing through the window, and would know that she very soon would need to have sex, for she always needed to have sex when she was sad, and was by turns ecstatically happy and inconsolably sad throughout each day.

She baked bread and made soups; she took a French course at City College and started speaking at times with the slightest French accent. Her instructor, a peroxide blond Frenchwoman in her thirties whose most memorable features were her unabashed black roots and furry black armpits, had once shared a taxi with Sartre. From the first day of class, Louanna worshiped her, and all things French.

I loved Louanna in my fashion, which is to say obsessively and falsely. I loved my idea of loving her, of course, my idea of love, and therefore I loved only an extension of myself. I'm not saying that this is how all nineteen-year-old males necessarily love, only that that is how I did, how I loved that particular woman at that time of our lives.

For brief hours I pulled away from her, from that violent arc of joy to despair and back and back which was her almost hourly shuttle along the track of our days, and I walked the streets of Coronado, always arriving at the beach. I'd been poor most of my life, adopted just a few years earlier into a middleclass family; I'd stopped thinking myself poor only recently. Still, all the wealth of Coronado, the rich sprawling beachfront houses, the perfect lawns, awed and intimidated me, though as I passed them, barefoot over the cooling cement, somehow they also belonged to me, were about me. A thousand sprinklers plugged permanently into the ground would flutter on after sunset, hissing secrets about grass and shrub, palm and eucalyptus, and of course as far as I was concerned, about me, for everything was about me.

Especially the ocean. I'd walk the waterline for hours, back and forth from the Del to the North Island fence, the same route as the UDT and SEAL team, and sometimes they passed me on their evening runs, at the same pace as their morning and afternoon runs, and I'd try to make eye contact with them, but no one looked at anything but the shaved head in front of him, or if he were in front he kept his stare fixed on the distant goal, the fence going north, the boulders of the Del, south.

Or I'd watch the surfers in their shiny black wetsuits mounting swells, working them or getting upended. I'd never surfed, never wanted to, primarily because I was a poor swimmer, and otherwise simply didn't fit in with the culture of water. I didn't love the ocean enough to want to be in it constantly, always to smell of it, taste it, be permanently concerned with its disposition, to live my life according to the tides. Still, it was about me. The ocean would have screeched to a halt had I not from time to time stared into it, screeched to a stop or simply grown bored with its own machinations, and sad. I was sole proprietor of so much sadness.

When I'd return from healing the ocean by my presence, after dark, to Louanna, she'd be pulling loaves from the oven, miniature loaves she'd frozen over the weekend for that week, different flavors, cheese loaves, herbal loaves, dried tomato and basil. She'd cook split pea soup and I'd smell it as I approached the golden porch light of the door. I'd change into my gee as she puttered in the kitchen, whispering French.

I'd do my fifty-minute drill: a thousand punches, five hundred front snap kicks with each leg. The formal exercises: Two, Three and Five, then Tamati Basai. In the dances, the kata, fighting was beautiful, because the attackers were ghosts, and I could read their thoughts. I moved through the kata like a smooth vanquisher of shadows and ghosts in the yellow light of the porch.

I'd take a shower before supper, negotiating around all her things, the ordered stuff of her "toilette," trying not to disrupt that order because I knew how much it meant to her, things being perfectly in place in that room where she spent hours applying makeup or weeping, and where twice she'd halfheartedly tried to kill herself.

Towards the end of my life with Louanna (in a couple of months I'd run twenty kilos to Grand Forks, North Dakota, and she'd take up with a French lounge singer she'd enchant in Mission Valley while I was gone), I met Mikey, her ex-husband. She'd needed to go over to his place to sign some papers, taxes or something. He lived in Ocean Beach in a little bungalow a few blocks from the water. I accompanied her because I needed to see him, this man Louanna loved but who could not have sex with her because his head was filled with horrors.

We took the bus because my '67 Mercury station wagon wasn't running, or maybe Barney had won it yet again in a poker game, or maybe we'd just decided the bus would be okay. I quizzed her about him from Coronado to Horton Plaza in downtown San Diego, where we transferred. And I kept pressing her.

She was somber, even a little sad. She wore a pink shirt knotted under her breasts so her tanned midriff showed. I asked her if she was sad because we were going to her old house. She said no, that didn't make her sad, that she wasn't sad at all, but I told her she seemed sad.

I'm just thinking, she said.

What are you thinking about? I asked, but didn't really want to know, and she knew I didn't. The sun hung over the ocean in the midst of its long, slow plunge through afternoon. But I pressed, as I always pressed, because I couldn't just sit quietly on a bus. I couldn't just sit quietly with her. She let me hold her hand, and stared out the window. There were only a few other people going to Ocean Beach on that bus, and they sat near the back.

What are you thinking about? I asked again.

I was trying to think in French, she said. I knew she was always practicing French in her head.

What were you thinking in French? I asked.

I was thinking a poem, she sighed, and turned her head in my direction to look out the other side of the bus, toward the beaches. She had a slightly crossed right eye, so sometimes, from certain angles, I couldn't tell when she was looking at me or beyond.

I was barefoot. I went everywhere barefoot. It was a karate thing. I hung my skinny legs over the seat in front of us. *A French poem? Who wrote it?*

I was writing it, in my head, she told me, and I felt bad for having interrupted her.

I pointed out to her, though, that she never wrote poems in English, and she said that she only wanted to make them in French. She'd been born and grew up in the Midwest. She'd never even been in the Eastern Time Zone. Her teacher was the only French person she'd ever met. I suddenly became angry at her for speaking sometimes with a French accent, and angry at the entire nation of France. At City College, I'd search for her after our classes; she'd be walking with her teacher, a woman ten years older and six inches shorter than she; the black tufts of the Frenchwoman's pits blossomed and were crushed and blossomed again as she gesticulated and Louanna beamed in the intensity of her regard. They jangled in swift though rudimentary French until they'd come upon me and switch to English.

I was angry but hardly ever let her know. She'd gotten another letter from her father earlier in the day, and I knew she was edgy from it. Her father was a preacher in the Midwest, and did not approve of me. He didn't approve of anything west of the Rockies, but he especially didn't approve of me, for I was the reason his daughter would burn in hell. He told Louanna in the letters he wrote weekly that she should stay with her husband.

I'd asked Louanna if her father knew why she'd left Mikey, and she'd wept for hours, so from that time forward I'd not broached the subject.

The sun was at about four o'clock. I didn't own a watch, but I could tell time from the sun pretty well. I asked Louanna if she loved me. She smiled and said sure, she loved me. She touched my cheek and then hugged my neck and I wanted to ask her if she loved me the way she loved Mikey. Instead, I asked her if she wanted to have sex. She laughed and said sure, she wanted to. She said when we got back to Coronado we would.

He was shorter than I, thirtyish, with straight blond hair he wore past his shoulders. He had a large handlebar in which his mouth was lost, like David Crosby's. His eyes, clear and blue, didn't seem particularly sad. He shook my hand, and because I'd lived some years around the Navy I almost called him sir. He smiled at me; that is, his massive mustache opened like something that lolls at the bottom of the ocean, and his teeth were revealed. Perhaps I smiled back, but was certainly too nervous to mean it.

I sat on the slab porch with him, drinking a beer, while Louanna moved about the kitchen as though it were still her own, making tea and knowing where everything was, and then sat down at the kitchen table and began filling out the forms.

I babbled and he listened, smiling, shaking his head in affirmation. I sipped my beer and tried not to look at him as I chattered. I smoked a cigarette, flicking ashes that hadn't formed yet, flicking, flicking, sucking, blathering, swigging. He nodded and smiled.

I had to take a piss, and said so. I stubbed out my cigarette on the cement step and left it there to light again when I returned. He pointed over his shoulder with his chin, and told me to bring him a beer when I came back, and to get myself another. As I passed, Louanna remained fixed upon the form she was filling out.

It was a woman's bathroom, one that a woman may deign to allow a male to share with her, but which was wholly appropriated to her tastes and needs. It was like the bathroom I shared with Louanna. The same brands of creams and bath oils lined the shelf below the cabinet, the same Dove and Prell the ledge of the tub. There was a framed ocean sunset over the toilet, and I stared into it, then zipped, washed my hands, looked for his razor, his deodorant, his stuff.

It was all tucked out of sight in the bottom drawer of the cabinet under the sink, in a shoe box: toothbrush and Crest, aerosol deodorant, silver Schick razor, Gillette blades, English Leather.

On the door was a poster of another sunset and a poem by Rod McKuen hung in its sky. I looked around for crud or pubic hairs, but could find none. The small room was pristine; the porcelain shone, the glass of the mirror was unsmudged.

We swigged our fresh Millers; I relit my Winston butt. He asked me about karate. Louanna had told him I gave private lessons, that I could break rocks with my hand. I said yeah, I could do that, but it's no big deal. He asked me to show him.

Louanna came out and talked a few details with him, official stuff I didn't understand. Then she hugged and petted him. The shadow of a palm tree stretched in the late afternoon light across the porch. Roses and fuchsia mingled along the low chain-link fence. A tiny herb garden flourished between the white posts of the patio overhang. They put their heads together and spoke in half-whispers for several minutes. They were so comfortable. As shadows grew and they stood hugging and whispering, I wanted to leave her there with him. I wanted to tell him how sorry I was that his head was packed with horrors. I wanted to go into the bathroom and drag all his stuff out of the bottom drawer and set it on the sink where it belonged.

Does it hurt? he asked. They had their arms around each other, looking at me. They were smiling. *When you break bricks. Does it hurt your hand?*

I looked at my right hand, opened and closed it. Yeah, it hurt, but I was used to it, that particular pain. But I said no, it didn't hurt. That was the easiest answer.

KILLING JUAN GOMEZ
FALL, 1972

Hal Harrison wanted me to kill Juan Gomez. He said he'd give me five thousand dollars if I killed him, two thousand five hundred if I just really messed him up.

Hal's father was a captain, my uncle/stepfather—whom I'd not seen much since moving out of his house on my eighteenth birthday—a lieutenant commander, so Hal outranked me. He was my age but much smarter, at least cagier. He had seven siblings, and the Harrison brood occupied a huge house near the golf course and the bay. Hal had a ham radio setup in his basement, and was the first serious cocaine dealer on Coronado Island. The second serious cocaine dealer on Coronado was Juan Gomez, a former SEAL, and an untouchable narc who played rugby, mangled anyone who crossed him, and parlayed his narc status into a nice little Coronado/Imperial Beach/Chula Vista/National City dealership. Hal said Juan had ripped him off for ten grand.

Hal assumed that because I smashed bricks with my hand at keg parties, and because I'd been teaching karate on Coronado for several years and had a reputation, and because I smoked a lot of dope and hung out at Dirty Dan's, I might consider killing Juan Gomez.

I knew even then that I was a pussy. Oh, I was pretty tough. I smashed bricks and rocks. I'd gotten into fights and messed guys up some, but managed to avoid ever tangling with a real man.

Juan Gomez was a real man, which is to say someone who had killed at least one other human being. Though no one could document how and when Juan Gomez had achieved this status, the mere fact that he'd been a SEAL on active duty in Vietnam meant that he had to have done so.

Hal drove a gray Mercedes. He slowed on C Avenue, rolled down his window, invited me into his car.

He didn't hedge. He flat out said he wanted me to kill Juan Gomez. He wanted me to do it with my hands, smash his head like a brick. Hal was quite nice about it. He told me to take a few days to think it over. I even tried to explain to Hal that I was a pussy, someone incapable of killing another human being, on purpose, anyway, but he wouldn't hear it. He just laughed, patted me on the shoulder while he steered his Mercedes, and told me to think about it.

With five thousand dollars I could quit working at the geedunk on the Amphibious Base for a whole year; for a whole year I wouldn't have to stack or unstack another chair; sweep, mop and buff another floor. I wouldn't have to teach karate to guys who got disappointed that I didn't show them secret killer "moves" the first lesson. I could flee the garage-apartment I slept in and buy a decent car, maybe even a nice used van. Hell, if I invested in a few kilos of weed, I could finish out the Seventies without working. The more I thought about it, the better killing Juan Gomez sounded.

Yet I knew, really knew, that I couldn't do it. But even with this knowledge I couldn't help working out how I'd do it. From the midst of pure subjunctive, I spent several days planning Juan Gomez's assassination.

I stalked him a little, watched and studied him from a distance. I knew that after playing rugby late Saturday afternoons at Star Park near the north end of the beach, the guys and their girlfriends and wives all went to Mexican Village and got soggy with margaritas. Still wearing their grass-stained rugby clothes, stinking and dirty, they'd spend hours laughing and drinking until someone slapped his girlfriend, or an arm-wrestling match got ratcheted up to haymakers in the parking lot. Juan Gomez was the boss of the crowd and always the drunkest and last to leave. He always had an argument with his girlfriend, the bartender told me, and sometimes sent her home in a cab so he could go shack up somewhere else.

He was just under six feet tall and weighed about two thirty. He was pumping iron when not a lot of other guys were doing it. He'd actually made it through UDT and onto the SEAL team. And he'd done at least one tour in Vietnam. He was in his late twenties and hugely handsome, with a thick black mustache and big scary dark eyes. His laugh was sinister, and he laughed constantly. SEAL was tattooed across the knuckles of his right hand.

He knew who I was. He found me amusing. He'd laugh and shake his head when he saw me, but didn't say anything, or said, "How's it hanging, sinsai," real low and wrapped in a chuckle, almost under his breath. He knew my kind, the officers' brats who spent their fathers' entire tours of duty in the base gyms, getting free and excellent instruction from the best Japanese sinsais the strong Yankee dollar, forked over by Special Services, could buy, while the sailors and marines came and went, from the States and then, after a few months, out to sea or directly to Vietnam. Most of the swabs weren't around enough to take more than a few lessons, which counted for nothing. I didn't register strongly enough with Juan Gomez for him to be contemptuous, but to the extent he even considered me, that was the general direction of his regard.

Which should have made it easier for me to kill him, but it didn't. After the first flush of excitement, it became difficult even to plan his execution. But this generally was how I thought I'd do it:

One Saturday he'd leave the Mexican Village just after 2 a.m. when it closed. He'd leave just ahead of the bartender, and I'd follow him from half a block back. He'd probably have ridden over from Star Park with one of his buds, so would be walking, or staggering. His girlfriend's apartment was on G or H a couple of blocks from the high school, so if he were going there and not somewhere else to shack up, he'd probably cut down Fourth and then turn onto G. Somewhere between Seventh and Eighth, where it would be darkest, I'd clobber him with a baseball bat, but not hard enough to kill him, because now I was resigned to earning only two thousand five hundred, at least enough to buy a nice used van. After I knocked him down, I'd whack his knees. The main thing was that there was no way I'd go after Juan Gomez empty-handed. My karate training had certainly not made me a killer, but it had made me much more aware, better aware than most, of my physical limitations. I knew what could happen if I tried to whack Juan Gomez without a weapon: I'd come up behind him and punch him hard in the back of his neck, and if he were really drunk he'd stagger forward and maybe fall to a knee, at which point I'd pop him a couple more times and maybe, maybe then he'd be on Queer Street. But just as likely the first punch, especially since he wouldn't be plugged into the ground like a Makiwara punching board but moving in the same direction as the blow, would just anger him, wake him up, even, and he'd wheel around and destroy me. No, if I were going to do this, I'd have to get a bat.

It would be several months before I'd live with Louanna on Orange Avenue. Barney and Phil came over to my hovel on Sixth Street, my sorry hutch, to enlist my help with a project. We couldn't all fit in the room without sitting on the bed, and none of us felt particularly cozy in bed with two other guys, even though we had our clothes on, so we took a walk.

Barney and Phil wanted me to help them roll some sailors. Phil needed money for the prom. He'd graduated a couple years previously, but his girlfriend was a senior, and wanted him to take her, so he needed some cash fast, and figured rolling sailors on payday might be the best way to get some.

I reminded them that my real father had done a lot of hard time, and that I didn't particularly want to follow his example. I could tell Barney's heart wasn't in the project, but Phil was wild-eyed, obsessed with rolling sailors for their payday cash. I told him I had other things on my mind, and didn't want to hear any more talk about rolling sailors. But how did he plan to do it? I asked. Where did he plan to do it?

Sailors were scum, at least the ones who weren't UDT or SEAL. A common insult had someone's sister screwing a sailor. Another common insult was simply to call someone a swab, a swabby. There was much talk of rolling sailors, but I doubted that anyone, anyone I knew, anyway, had ever done it.

But considering my own dark project, I was curious as to how Phil was planning his. He babbled something about lurking around the main gate of North Island, but as soon as he said that, I didn't bother to listen to the money end of his plan. If he were going to jump some guys on the street in front of the main gate, with armed guards standing right there snapping salutes to the cars coming and going at all hours, he was definitely on his own.

But he had some hash and a pipe, so I walked with him and Barney to the beach, and as the sun was going down we smoked about a quarter of a gram. Then Barney fired up a joint.

We passed three other guys smoking a joint, and we two threesomes acknowledged one another with big grins in that dull-witted fellowship of the stoned.

"Got some righteous shit here, man," one of them said, stopping to pass his righteous shit to Barney, who took it and toked.

Even as raked as we were on Lebanese hash, we could tell that what the guy was turning us on to was at another level. He said it was Thai stick, the best, the best fucking ever, that he'd gotten it right there from the monkey's mouth just a couple of months ago.

I'd heard about the stuff. This was great. It rolled right over the hash and Barney's lame joint and repeatedly licked our sticky brains.

As the six of us floated along we kind of talked and laughed but none of it made any sense, which was fine. The air was dark but for the moon and the hazy glow of street lamps on the other side of the border of boulders a couple hundred yards from the waterline; we followed the waterline toward the North Island fence, laughing and chortling non-sequiturs, but I knew something was happening, something was taking shape.

Phil was paired up with the little one, the little swab who'd turned us on to the Thai stick and who was pulling out another joint of it; the little swab wore a ridiculous Hawaiian shirt and his red hair was slicked back. In the moonlit gloom one could still make out a crimson batch of zits cascading down his chin onto his neck, though his face was oddly clear of them. Phil was going to jump him any second. And I could tell that Barney knew that Phil was getting ready to pounce on the little one. Barney and I made eye contact, and even in that dimness, even as ripped as we were, we communicated. We acknowledged to each other that we knew what was happening.

Barney was paired with a goofy black guy, a cartoonishly skinny guy who was hunched over and who laughed on cue but said nothing though he seemed to be mumbling constantly, even when someone else was talking. I was paired with a white guy who looked like he'd just been elected vice-president of the chess club. He squinted such that his thick black-rimmed glasses seemed not to be working. Barney's and mine wore identical white shirts with buttoned-down collars.

I wanted to signal to Phil to cool it, not to jump the little swab, but I didn't know how. So I just blurted out, "Phil, don't," but no one acted like he'd heard me, not even Barney, so I said, "Phil, don't do it," but again it was like I hadn't said anything; the little swab was telling a story with lots of hand jive. He was cracking himself up, pinching the joint and trying to pass it to Phil. I knew that Phil would at least wait until the joint was finished, but it was down pretty low already, or at least seemed so in the dark, making red trails on the air as the little swab gesticulated about a girl back home in Bumfuck, Texas, or Idaho. Phil wasn't swinging his arms at all as he walked beside the little swab.

The four of us just stood there, struck dumb, as Phil clawed in the sand for the little guy's wallet. He held him face down, and the little swab just gasped and grunted and Phil tugged at his wallet, which was securely wedged into the back pocket of tight jeans.

Barney figured he had no choice, so shoved his swab and jumped on top of him; the skinny guy went down like he was expecting it, was wondering what had taken Barney so long to catch on. But then Barney seemed not to know what to do next. He didn't go for the guy's wallet. He just pinned him in the sand and stared up at Phil digging desperately at the little swab's back pocket.

I swept the legs out from under mine, and just stood over him. His glasses came off; I picked them up and handed them to him. I didn't know why I'd put him down, but it had something to do with tribal solidarity. It had something to do with loyalty.

Neither Barney nor I, nor our downed sailors, spoke; all four of us just watched Phil dig at the little sailor's ass, until someone, Barney or I, said, "Cool it, Phil," and walked over and dragged him off the little sailor.

Phil didn't resist. He seemed to realize how incredibly stupid he looked digging at the guy's ass, and had simply been waiting for someone to help him stop looking that stupid. Barney mumbled an apology, and so did I, and all three swabs stayed on the ground, said nothing, just breathed hard, as we stumbled toward the lights beyond the boulders.

I watched Juan Gomez and his buddies play rugby, and it was cool because sometimes a dozen or so people would just sit on the grass and watch. None of the players cared or even really noticed. Juan Gomez was the meanest son-of-a-bitch in the game; he relished hurting his friends and laughing at their discomfort. They all laughed, but they were all very serious, too. The game meant something to all of them, somehow affirmed and connected them. Several were off-duty cops from Imperial Beach; a couple were active-duty SEALs. One was a well-known local speed dealer, a guy who waited tables as a kind of lame cover, and as a way to kill time and socialize; it seemed that semi-big-time dealing was not particularly demanding or time-consuming, just nerve-wracking, and the game must have been one way to take the edge off.

As a kid I'd not been beaten a lot, which is to say not daily, but when I'd gotten a beating it had been severe, what they now call "abusive." We'd lived on the highways of American, my father thieving, kiting checks and stealing cars for—I guess one may say—a living. He was wanted at one point in over forty states before he was caught and put in prison. The second time he was released from prison, just a few days after returning to us, he'd gotten drunk and punched me in the face with all his force, knocking me out.

I watched those real men playing rugby, and of course I was high. I watched them and thought of my father, probably back in prison again, and I thought of my good uncle/stepfather, how formal and manly he looked in his dress blues, how proud he was to be an officer and a gentleman. And I thought about my favorite karate dance, the kata named Tamati Basai, in which you stand at the center of the world, and six men who do not exist attack you in an orderly fashion, and you respond perfectly, vanquishing, gracefully and stylishly, absolutely nothing.

DIRTY DAN'S
FALL, 1972

Dave and Rocky smoked pot all day in Dirty Dan's garage bedroom. Dirty Dan, Dave's older brother, wasn't around much, and let them use his bedroom, which was the family garage converted into the kind of space a young male could occupy comfortably. Dave sat in a tattered burgundy overstuffed chair rolling and passing around joints from about eleven in the morning to nine in the evening on Mondays, Wednesdays, and Fridays during the school year; on Tuesday and Thursday afternoons he attended classes at Southwestern Community College. Weekends he didn't move from his chair except to piss on his mother's roses. Rocky attended UCSD for a while but quit, started up again, and quit again. Then he transferred to Southwestern.

Rocky was the smart one, Dave the sage. They'd smoke joint after joint and Rocky would gush interesting information about Led Zeppelin and Ten Years After and Rod Stewart. Dave nodded and offered laconic though sage color. They were a team. I thought of them that way. Dave and Rocky. Never Rocky and Dave. Dave was the boss. It was his crazy brother's room. He sat in the big chair. He rolled the joints, always.

And Rocky, though he was the smart one, the talker, wouldn't have had it any other way. He was a born sidekick and seemed happy to have been thus fated. Dave was the boss of his soul, and that was cool.

Dave, I'd eventually realize, was only an attitude with hair that flowed past his shoulders and a gift for seeming wise, but with the actual thought capacity of a goldfish. In the early Seventies, though I assumed as everyone else did that he was a fool, I also thought that he was as sage as he seemed. I thought that somehow his smoking all that pot had made him so. To some extent it had. I'd simply mistaken vacuity for sagacity.

Dave's big ambition was to be a rock star. Rocky's big ambition was for Dave to be a rock star. Sometimes Dave stopped rolling joints and picked up a guitar and started strumming and whining one of his original compositions. He never played anything but songs he'd written, and he never asked if anyone wanted to hear them. He'd just stop rolling joints and pick up his guitar, tune it a minute, turn off the stereo, and start strumming and whining. I sometimes wondered when Dave had time actually to write his songs. He seemed so busy rolling joints and weaving laconic commentary around Rocky's chatter, and playing and whining his songs about Sandy, with whom Dave was famously in love.

She was incredibly attractive and had graduated the same year as he and Rocky from Coronado High, two years ahead of me. She was blonder than blond, bombshell endowed and pretty as a movie star. She was a California cliché from a distance, but down-to-earth and decent up close, which Dave never got. He required her, from the moment he saw her, to be at a distance.

And over the years, as she caught wind of his obsession with her, his endless songs of love and longing, she was glad to remain there. She was constantly fending off jokes at parties; people would howl with laughter and sing snatches of Dave's songs they'd heard over at Dirty Dan's garage-bedroom. She was always a trooper, laughing along, but I figured it had to get to her. Indeed, I could tell that it was getting to her by how forced her laughter seemed. And she wore much too much make-up, which was fine for being looked at from a distance, but up close its effect was that nuances in facial expressions were more pronounced, and therefore easier to read.

Like the ones who laughed at Dave's songs and sang snatches of them at parties to tease Sandy, I kept going over to Dirty Dan's to smoke pot with Dave and Rocky. The price of the dope was listening to Dave strum and whine, and that didn't seem like much. Dave and Rocky were oddly revered. People goofed on them, but also admired them for their consistency. Dirty Dan's garage bedroom was a retreat where you could always go at particular times to get high. Dave and Rocky would always be there, would always be doing and saying the same things. Rather like church, which nobody attended.

The ocean was two blocks away. Granite boulders stacked in a jaggedly elegant fence along the length of the beach separated it from Ocean Boulevard; they were blue gray in the slants of sunlight, morning then evening. Shadows oozed from them, especially after the sun plunked and the street lamps snapped on. I'd listen to Dave/Rocky and their music, smoke their dope then wander off to the beach.

When I walked the beach in the evenings after getting high at Dirty Dan's, I thought a lot about being in love, because as far as I could tell I'd never been (though I was weeks away from falling into something with Louanna). I could imagine it, and what I imagined was beyond music, certainly beyond what Dave strummed and whined about Sandy.

I didn't just want to get laid; I'd done that. I wanted to fall in love, like Dave, but not at a distance. I thought I wanted intimacy, but had absolutely no idea what that was. I probably had a better idea of what love was, at least the obsessive insane kind I imagined and would soon act out with Louanna.

I didn't realize how lonely I'd become. I had friends, a network of acquaintances, workmates at the geedunk. People liked that I'd smash bricks and rocks with my hand at parties when they asked me to; they liked that I'd fight anyone, anytime, though no one on Coronado wanted to fight me, and I really didn't want to fight any of them. There were rumors, only a couple of them almost true, about my getting into fights in Tijuana and Imperial Beach, taking on gangs of drunk Mexicans.

But I had little in common with other young people in Coronado. They were all rich by the standards of my childhood. Even my stepparents were almost rich by those standards. I saw things differently, though I didn't realize how differently. My assumptions about how the world works were profoundly different from those of everyone I knew.

For one thing, I didn't feel as safe as everyone else seemed to feel, as at ease under the sun, under the moon and stars that wheeled over Coronado. I didn't feel in danger; I didn't feel that there was anyone or anything on Coronado that would harm me. I just never felt at home anywhere on the island, not in my stepparents' house, or in my hovel, or at Dirty Dan's. On the beach at night, high, after walking the couple of blocks from Dirty Dan's, I'd scare myself, cruising the waterline. I'd consider what would happen if I trudged out into the waves and drowned. Everyone at Dirty Dan's would be kind of bummed for a couple of days, maybe, but nothing would change. Dave wouldn't stop rolling joints and Rocky wouldn't stop chattering. The people I worked with at the geedunk would shake their heads and stare into their coffee mugs after the lunch shift. But then they'd hire someone else to sweep, mop, and buff the linoleum six days a week. My stepparents would be pissed but relieved. A few peers would feel creepy for an hour or two.

But no one would weep. I was certain, and was probably correct, that no one would weep if I died. I'd become like one of the legendary OD's, the girl who got some heroine and shot too much the first time, the guy who took a whole bottle of Quaaludes. They got mentioned, referenced in conversations, casually, from time to time, but not even as cautionary tales, more in the spirit of bragging, a kind of youth-culture badge of civic honor, proof that Coronado was cool, too, because bad things had happened there, dark stuff just like in Chula Vista.

I was connected to nothing on the island, no place. Dave, Dirty Dan and their younger brother would own the house in whose garage Dave now held services with his stoned acolytes. Everyone I knew was rooted in the hardpan, the tight rocky dirt of the island. Everyone had familial connections that were real and enduring, not phony like mine. Everyone else was at home there.

I didn't feel sorry for myself, just not completely safe. Perhaps I thought that falling in love was finding a home in someone else's life, finding that particular safety. Maybe I was that naïve. Maybe I was right.

Someone had brought over a healthy wad of blond hash to Dirty Dan's, and six of us had smoked it in Rocky's bong. I was in the red zone, stoned out of time, and walked the waterline, as always barefoot (because going everywhere barefoot was part of my karate persona, and because I owned only one pair of shoes, orange sneakers I wore to work in the geedunk). There were two or three bonfires along the beach. The Hotel Del Coronado was a glittering hulk of shadow a half mile south. There was a lull in the landing and takeoff cycles of fighter jets, supply planes, and humpbacked AWAC's onto the North Island Naval Air Station's several airstrips. They moaned over the beach unceasingly through the day and deep into night except for such lulls as that moment, and in that quiet, in that dark bass note of ocean, I saw a figure standing in the foam, wearing an iridescent white dress that draped to her ankles. She seemed dressed for a wedding, but not as the bride, rather as a bridesmaid or maid of honor. Her shoes stood beside her.

She smoked a cigarette, sucking it hard and often. She stood with her arms crossed, rubbing her palms over what I imagined in the dark to be goose flesh, flicking her cigarette when she wasn't sucking it. She stared into the dark water as though she expected something to happen there, something that wasn't now happening: the slow grind of low tide.

When I was close enough to be heard without shouting, I said hi.

Her name was Mickey or Terry or Lou, one of those names that can go either way. She'd been on a date and the guy had slipped her some acid, had laughed, telling her, as she was coming on, that he'd slipped it in her beer. She'd never dropped. She was scared but being tough about it. She'd told the guy to fuck off and then had run to the beach. She'd been standing there for over an hour, she thought, but wasn't sure. I told her she should probably keep moving. I told her I'd walk her to the Del and sit on the rocks with her and smoke a joint, that the joint would take some of the edge off.

She said she'd never smoked dope. I was incredulous; not only had I never heard of anyone dropping acid before ever smoking pot, but also I'd never met a peer who hadn't toked, not on Coronado, anyway.

She said that Jesus was her Savior, and that she was high on Him. I said that no, she was actually, right that second, high on acid, and that she probably needed something to take the edge off, so I'd turn her on over on the boulders behind the Del. She insisted that she didn't need anything else, that Jesus would help her through all this, that Jesus had probably sent me to help her. Yeah, He sent me with this joint, I told her, plucking it from my shirt. She picked up her shoes, flicked the remnant of the cigarette she'd sucked down to the filter into the dark over the water, gazing after the tiny red sparks as they sprayed upon the breeze and blinked out.

As we walked over the wet sand I tried to pry vital info from her tripping head. Her father was some flavor of admiral, rear or vice or even full, and her mother was a bitch. She'd been going with the guy who'd slipped her the acid for over five months. They were engaged. He was half Mexican and her mother hated him, but not enough to tell her father he was half-Mexican, yet. He was actually very religious, had helped her find Jesus, but had wanted her to convert to Catholicism, not have a personal relationship with Jesus. He was really a great guy, but had been hanging out lately with dudes in Mission Beach who just surfed and did drugs. It was only a phase, though, Jesus testing their love.

I asked her why a God who would allow American jets to drop sticky fire on Asian children, who would allow Nazis to murder millions of Jews, would give a flying fuck about her relationship with Pedro. She said his name was Lesley or Francis, like hers one of those that can go either way.

This went on for hours. Until dawn. We sat on the granite behind the Del, facing the ocean, hidden from the beach by the boulders, the palms flapping languidly in the floodlights from the hotel behind us. She praised Jesus; I refuted her claims. I smoked the joint, and the flattened roach of powerful Panama Red I had in my wallet. She was clearly on one hell of a trip, and seemed actually to be enjoying it. She talked and talked. I tried to wedge into the wall of her words, but was too stoned to keep up with her. I'd respond to things she'd said minutes earlier, and she'd pause, wrinkle her brow, then push on. At one point she announced that she had to pee. I actually got scared that she'd leave me, trudge back to the hotel and then, after peeing, simply go off after Lesley or Francis, or just go home.

But she pulled up her long white gown, peeled down her panties, and, squatting over the spray from waves beating below us, didn't stop talking about Jesus.

She was the first pretty girl I'd not wanted, particularly, to have sex with. And yet I couldn't stand the idea of her leaving me. I told her about my mother who was dying of multiple sclerosis but I didn't know where; I told her about my brothers and sister I'd not seen in five years, about my father who was probably in prison again, about growing up in cars all over America until my father got caught, about getting adopted and then living in Japan where I studied karate, and then coming to Coronado. I was stoned and dawn was revving up and I told her everything, and she told me everything, and everything was about Jesus and how much she hated her mother.

I told her everything and she heard nothing, and that was fine. I told her she should eat something, I should eat something. We had to go to the Nite & Day on Orange Avenue and eat Three Eggers.

We both drank lots of ice water. Trudy filled our glasses seven or eight times. I had my eggs with extra hashbrowns and extra toast.

"What are you going to do with your life?" she asked me. No one had ever asked me that. I'd never asked myself. I figured Soviet missiles would take care of the future, and said so.

"But what if that doesn't happen? What'll you do?"

Her white dress was even more stunning in the daylight. It had delicate embroidery around the sleeves and along the neckline. She wore a little eyeliner, and it was faded, as was her lipstick. She stared hard at me, and I fixed on the smear of yolk at the corner of her mouth.

"I want to fall in love," and it was the first thing I'd said to her that I immediately regretted having said.

"As a career?" she replied, and it was the first witty thing she'd said to me, and we laughed for the first time.

"No, I was thinking more in terms of a hobby," I answered, and we laughed some more.

"I hope you find Jesus," she said.

"I hope you find another boyfriend," I said. "And another mother."

She walked down Orange Avenue, north, in the direction of the bay, dangling her shoes at her side from two fingers. Then she turned right at Seventh and disappeared.

I waited a few hours, walked around, read in the library, and then headed over to Dirty Dan's. Dan was actually there. He was dripping something onto a cloth, then shaking it in a big plastic bag. Then he put the bag to his mouth and "whooped" the chemical on the cloth, sucking and blowing into the bag numerous times such that the hyperventilating had to be part of the high. He passed the bag to Rocky; Rocky whooped and passed it to Dave; Dave whooped and passed it to Steve; Steve whooped and passed it to somebody I didn't know, who whooped and passed it to someone else I didn't know, who whooped and tried to hand it to me. I said no, that I drew the line at the active ingredient in airplane glue. Everyone got a big kick out of that, and Dave rolled a joint.

Then Dan asked Dave to sing his new song about Sandy. Dan was the only person who ever actually asked to hear his brother sing, and did it just so he could laugh at him, and by laughing, literally rolling on the funky red carpet that was clotted with seeds and flecks of weed, give everyone else permission to laugh as well.

But Dave always picked up his guitar from behind the chair and strummed and whined, and Dan always laughed his ass off and told his brother he'd balled Sandy eighty times, and so had all his buddies, and then he'd describe a typical encounter with her, what he'd done to her and how she'd responded. Dan had no particular gift for narrative, but he made up for that lack with a true performer's panache, which included much pantomime.

Dan had long greasy black hair and a fuck-you mustache. He had a black patch over his left eye and it seemed he always had a cast on some part of one of his arms that he wielded like a weapon, which of course it was. Dan never wore a shirt, and he wasn't particularly muscular but big-boned, and looked formidable half-naked. He could consume vast quantities of anything and not pass out. That was what he was mainly known for, that and getting in fights so ferocious that even when he lost his stock went up.

And of course after Dave finished his new song, a slow one about the time it took to love him, time to care, and she'd someday look for him and he'd not be there, or some such vacuous crap, and Dan went nuts in the middle of a whoop, rolled on the carpet cackling, yelping, and everyone, even Rocky, laughed, too, but I didn't laugh, that one time, I didn't laugh. I asked Dave if he really loved her. Then before he could goose the gerbil in his head to start running on its wheel, I answered my own question; I told him he couldn't possibly love her. If he loved her he wouldn't sing shit like that, and my saying so made Dan and everybody else bray even louder, and I hated their laughter, and just stared at Dave.

"What is she to you?" I asked.

"She's my muse," he said, almost weeping, I thought, but he was too stoned to have anything like a real emotion, and the idea of a muse was probably something he'd heard from Rocky.

"She's not your fucking muse," I said. "Rocky's your muse. What is she?" I pressed.

Dave reached over and cranked up the stereo. Eric Clapton wailed a lover's lament on KGB. In advance of love, in anticipation, my heart was already broken, though I wouldn't know for years.

My Ex-Stepfather
Autumn, 1971

He was an E7, a chief petty officer, when the Navy decided he was too smart not to be an officer, and sent him to Purdue to earn a degree in electrical engineering. Then they rolled him through Officer Candidate School and made him a lieutenant junior grade. He was a lieutenant commander when he retired with over thirty years in the service of his country, and almost as many in the service of his wife, the real boss of his soul.

It had been her idea, her idea entirely, to adopt my brother and me after knowing us only a month, that is to say, only a few weeks after our criminal father, her criminal brother, had dumped us in San Diego, but of course she'd consulted with her husband. She'd said she could handle one of us, me, but wasn't sure she could take on two in addition to the three younger kids she already had, and to his great credit, to the credit of his humanity, his entirely sweet nature, he told her it was both or neither. It was thus he saved my brother's life, and set him on a course to become likewise a spit-shined officer in the United States Navy.

Their marriage thrived because he wasn't around much. My aunt was a West Pac Widow, raising kids pretty much alone while her husband performed long stints of sea duty, long cruises upon the oceans of the world punctuated by raucous stints in foreign ports, and I can only hope that my ex-stepfather, my uncle by marriage, got very drunk and soundly laid often on those long tours. I don't want to think of him as having been unwaveringly faithful, under such circumstances, to such a woman.

I met her in 1967, and the first thing she did after feeding me was to reveal her vision of the world. She did this not in some grand speech, some formal declaration, but simply in how she lived and what she had to say, tersely, about world events. I was thirteen, but I immediately discerned I was in the charge of a stalwart American, which in a few years I would recognize, wrongly, as a neo-fascist with more or less murderous regard for most of the rest of the world, representatives of which occupied many of the neighborhoods not far—never far enough—from where she lived. But in my twenties I misjudged her. She wasn't a hater; she was just fiercely private, and classically conservative.

And my ex-stepfather was certainly no more liberal than she; but he'd been a Kennedy Democrat, so his embrace of right-wing ideology was less a matter of conviction than despair. His wife simply viewed the world in terms of right people and wrong people, and she and her like were right people, and all the rest were the wrong people. The right people took impeccable care of what was theirs, did not impinge upon what was not, and valued above all else that which is clean and ordered, and there was no higher value, not really, than cleanliness and orderliness, and

33

only the right people, who of course were a subset of white people, truly understood this. Japanese were honorary white people if only because they were clean and orderly, though certain defects, such as their not actually being white, diluted that prized status.

Both of my stepparents were great truth-tellers, except that they designated huge caches of information as That Which Should Not Under Any Circumstances Be Discussed; usually, but not always, this was personal family matters, ugly history, best left untouched in that great and cluttered attic of repressed memories. For example, it was okay for my stepmother to announce loudly and often how utterly full of shit I was, but it was not okay for me to probe her childhood, ask about what it had been like as her brother's—my father's—baby sister. She'd stiffen and cast me a kind of party line whenever I asked questions about her youth, about what had made her brother, beyond simply his whacked-out chemistry, such a sick man.

In their way, they were decent, humble people, especially my stepfather, who is dead. A second generation Swede from Nebraska, he'd spoken only Swedish the first years of his life. His mother died when he was six or seven, and that somehow caused him neither to speak nor eat for a long time. His father, a fireman as far as I could gather, soon remarried someone my stepfather came to love quite deeply, so he started eating and talking again. And that is all I know, all I was ever able to get out of him. He would sit at the dinner table with me for hours, talking—he loved to talk, to hold forth a little, about politics and history and proper conduct and sports—and everything was fine as long as we kept things fairly formal. He was patient with me when we conversed, and listened intently, but when he spoke he kept going and going, droning slowly, carefully, in a slow, soporific babble, a late summer creek of a flow of words, as he picked his teeth and stared off, a cup of coffee and cigarette anchoring him to the table, the blurry naked woman on his left arm poised to sachay into oblivion, the USN emblem on his other a stamp of institutional pride. At such times, when he sat and talked with me, just me, he was as good a father as a man can be, and I loved him accordingly.

But I never understood his devotion to my aunt, my stepmother, my tormentor, and in no small measure his tormentor, the tormentor of everyone around her, a circle she kept small and tight, manageable. I now know he was devoted because it was simply in his nature to be so, but also because he was of a generation that believed in it, believed in committing, putting one's life on a path early and then working hard to keep it there. His devotion was also born of guilt, the fact that he got to sail off and hang out with guys, do fun work, and she stayed home and took care of everything that wasn't riding the great waters; I think it was also born of the fact that that naked female on his arm meant he indeed had a libido, and at some period in his life, perhaps right into the sixties, fed it lavishly every time he sailed off, except when he became a commanding officer, albeit of the u.s.s Phoebe, an msc, Minesweeper Coastal, a tiny wooden ship of thirty officers and men that in the late sixties cruised between its home base of Sasebo, Japan, and the coast of Vietnam.

The North Island Naval Air Station billet, after Sasebo, was a kind of reward for spending so many years at sea. For the almost three years in Sasebo, I'd seen little of him, which hadn't been a big deal because I didn't know him, though the Woman Alone With Five Kids thing was being repeated in my life by virtue of his absence; in Sasebo, instead of being in a federal prison, the missing father was on a little wooden ship plucking explosives from the depths. Once again, I was the oldest of five children, though three of them I didn't know very well, yet liked just fine. The difference was that I wasn't poor, and as the son of a naval officer I acquired officer status. I knew exactly where I was in the social scheme and it was equal to my stepfather's rank, pretty far down within, though securely plugged into, the Elite Order.

On Coronado Island, he was around much more, and was rather morose for being so, given that my stepmother, anyway, characterized "shore duty" as a kind of blessed state they'd earned by years of suffering separation. From the time we arrived back in the States after almost three years in Sasebo, I had roughly twenty-two months until my eighteenth birthday, and so lived for the first time in my life for an extended period under what may be called normal circumstances: a man and woman and children living daily in one another's presence and constant regard in a single domicile.

I hated it. He hated it. She hated it. The younger ones would have hated it had they known to. What he hated, besides not being on the ocean, was being in close proximity to a seventeen-year-old male, something he'd not had to do since he was a chief petty officer, and there must truly be nothing more disgusting. She hated it because she would have hated any circumstance of mere family; she was a bright, strong, ambitious woman who loathed herself for being ambitious and not understanding why raising a family wasn't enough for her, would and could never be enough for one as intensely focused and smart as she. He'd never even wanted to be an officer; he'd loved being a sailor and just happened to be too good at it, so the Navy wanted him to do something else, but it was she who compelled him, who pushed and shamed him toward a modest success and status. His commission had been as much hers as his, and she should indeed have been a naval officer herself. She'd have made flag rank and whipped whole units of young men and women into shape.

Perhaps if she'd had two thousand young males to monitor and instruct, frighten and harden, instead of just two, she'd have been more successful. For, to the responsibility of raising us through adolescence she brought to bear a severity of purpose equal to the task of mentoring a battalion of hormone-crazed youths, but which was so out of proportion to what we required as to be abusive.

"You look like shit," "You're a phony," "I bet you think the girls are going to fall all over you," "You'll amount to nothing," "All your taste is in your mouth," "You look like an animal," "You act like an animal," "You're a coward," and the worst cut of all, "You're just like Dick," her brother, my biological father. Pretty innocuous stuff, except that it was unrelenting; every interaction included, almost without exception, an insult of some kind, not just a correction, an admonition, but a bitter personal slight, delivered always with clenched teeth or pursed lips, narrowed eyes. She did not disguise her hatred, and yet did not recognize it as such, and neither did he, constantly having to support her even when she was wrong, always loyally watching her parental back, silently concurring.

But then he would sit with my brother and me after the other children, the younger ones whom he had sired, had vacated the table and she was puttering about, complaining about how much I ate, about the little grunts and ticks my brother emitted as he tried to sit still but couldn't, and my uncle/stepfather would talk, talk, talk to us about anything we wanted to talk about, would listen to us and take what we said seriously, and would drone on and on and on in sentences that did not so much break down in structure as melt one into the next, about politics and sports and ideas, and at those moments, and on similar occasions when I returned to visit right up into my early forties and he was shrunken and frail, he was the only father I cared to claim.

So on my eighteenth birthday as I stood packed and ready to leave his house, I hoped I would get out the door and settled into my new home—a garage apartment so small I literally could not move in it except to wedge through the door and onto the bed, or wedge into the bathroom where the shower and toilet were hideous—before my stepfather returned from work. I didn't quite make it. He stood slack-jawed at the sight of me standing with my sloppily packed stuff around my feet, asked what I was doing. I informed him I'd found an apartment and would move into it that afternoon.

I couldn't wait to get out the door. I was legally free of that house, the insults it cost to be fed and sheltered there, free of my stepmother's palpable loathing.

My stepfather stood before me in his dress blues; he'd returned not just from work but something formal. His service ribbons told a story I understood a little: Good Service; Korea; Vietnam; four or five vague Acknowledgments of Competence, for showing up and not fucking up. One or two that indicated he was Above Average.

And I knew that the man standing before me was above average. I knew he was smart and humble, proud and decent. I knew that he tolerated me for love of a woman born to bust his balls, a woman stronger and brighter than he, certainly brighter than I. And I knew that he tolerated me because he'd come to have feelings for me similar to what a father has for a son, but also different if only because I was so different from him, on such a different path, for I was the actual son of a criminal, eldest spawn of the sick brother of his severe, sad wife. I was bad at math; I cared nothing for how things worked, except insofar as "things" were linguistic abstractions. I could not follow him into equations, into the joy of puzzles, the contentment of concrete solutions. I was wholly alien to everything he valued. And yet he'd watched me, somewhat at a distance, transform from a boy to something less than a man but not a boy; he'd talked talked talked to me after meals; he'd been sincere with me, and I with him, at least on occasion. I felt bound to this man by loss.

We both mourned mothers, and in the various worlds of men had to act tougher than we really were. Neither of us was by nature mean-spirited. I had a bit of a mean streak, when crossed could be exceedingly destructive in bursts, but did not, would never harbor a sustained loathing, and he didn't either.

I don't recall what he said, except that the words were all but mumbled and seemed to express some sadness. I think it wasn't that I was leaving, but that I looked ridiculous doing so, on my eighteenth birthday, the clutter of adolescent possessions at my feet, that made him sad. I must have looked doomed, utterly, and yet so hopeful and excited, a little scared. I couldn't wait to grow my hair long, to smoke dope all the time, to stay up as late as I wished, to have a place to take girls for sex. I couldn't wait to screw up everything, to quit high school and move to L.A. to write songs but end up selling herbal French cosmetics in East L.A. and Watts. I couldn't wait to get involved with a suicidal older woman who would screw my brains out. I couldn't wait to run twenty kilos of pot to Grand Forks, North Dakota, and escape incarceration only by the dumbest luck. I couldn't wait for the second insane intimacy of my life to result in a saline abortion. I couldn't wait to have part of my upper lip chewed off in a cowboy biker bar in San Bernardino. I couldn't wait to spend the next several years having pretty much indiscriminate sex and ingesting great quantities of hallucinogens. I couldn't wait to be an irresponsible little narcissist.

And I was packed and ready, my stuff in crinkled paper bags, most of my clothes in a battered suitcase, my books in two boxes, my "important papers" in a folder under my arm. My '67 Mercury station wagon was gassed up and ready to glide me and my worldly possessions a block and a half down the street, and that good man saw everything, even the hope in my face, and maybe he thought about the war that was still simmering, the one he felt personally responsible for his country screwing up because just a few months earlier he'd not been able to win it in his little wooden ship. And now he was seeing off this half-baked man into a famished world, this doughy, skinny, pretty boy packed with needs, desires, false dreams, and a small measure of dangerous intent. He stared at me a long few seconds, then turned away.

My Ex-Stepmother
Fall 2001, Fall 1974

I phoned her from my home in Prague three days after the events of September 11, 2001. My eleven-year-old Ema had mentioned "Bobbie Yo" at dinner, recalled something about our visiting the woman she vaguely regards as her American grandmother, or someone approximating such a relation. This time, my daughter didn't ask why we no longer visit Bobbie Yo, why we have no contact with her, even when we're back in the States. She simply recalled something about food, the way Bobbie Yo cooked something. She said nothing about the jets slamming into the great buildings, the fire and death she'd seen on TV, the changed world. She talked about the way a woman she'd not seen since she was four years old cooked turkey dressing.

That night I drank some hearty Moravian red called Frankovka, and watched a German station that was doing extended coverage on the horrors in New York and Washington. And I thought of Bobbie Yo, whom I called mother for thirty years, from the time she adopted my brother and me when I was almost fourteen and he was twelve. I phoned her at about two in the morning, which was five in the afternoon in California.

I announced myself; she paused, then said, "Why do you call? You don't want anything to do with me."

I told her she was right, but that my daughters deserved to have some sense of family in the States, and that she and I should try to reconfigure our regard for one another for their sake. Something else was blurted, then one of us hung up.

It had been stupid of me, emotionally stupid, to try to talk to her. I'd burned whatever we had been, down to nothing; nothing connected us now but indignation towards the other. She'd inserted herself into a conflict over money between my ex-wife and me, and had taken my ex-wife's side. She and my ex-wife, one of the most decent, honorable people I have ever known and someone who remains a friend, were flat out wrong, and my ex-wife would never have approved of her inserting herself into the conflict, anyway. My ex-wife and I resolved our dispute before our lawyers could suck any more money from the situation; my soon-to-be ex-stepmother owed me an apology and I insisted in no uncertain terms, and with a venom fermented over decades, that she express such a sentiment to me or simply kiss my ass.

We'd both been waiting years for something to strike a match to the last thread between us, an excuse to extricate ourselves from a relationship that was sick at its core. We'd disliked each other since I was in my early teens and she her early thirties, and had both felt guilt for disliking the other. I'd told myself that I loved her even though I didn't like her, but I never loved her. And yet the powerful feelings I've had for her are not strictly loathing, either. Or what I feel is a filial love clamped to a loathing that verges on the profound.

Ema called her Bobbie Yo because bobbie, or "babi" in Czech, is short for babicka, grandmother, and because my ex-stepmother would say "Yo, Ema," as a greeting, though I never quite understood why, since she'd not grown up in Brooklyn and had never greeted anyone else that way.

Just hours after a phone call from my adoptive mother in which she accused me of being unfair to my ex-wife and ordered me to desist; in other words, after she'd inserted herself in a wholly inappropriate way into a delicate, personal matter, I wrote her a letter that all but declared us divorced as mother and son, and it achieved precisely that condition. Divorcing my adoptive mother, I divorced, by extension, my adoptive father and two adoptive sisters as well, three people for whom I'd always held genuine affection. My ex-stepmother was the queen of their souls; where she erased her affections, they rubbed out theirs.

So, with one epistolary flourish, I subtracted any sense of American family from my daughters' lives, any sense but my oldest's vague though stubborn memories of an edgy woman who was boss of a big, lovely house in a place called Coronado, California.

She adopted my brother and me just a few weeks after meeting us. Our father had rushed us away from our dying mother and three younger siblings, and from numerous warrants for his arrest. He'd already done two five-to-ten-out-in-three stints in federal prisons, and was months away from his third incarceration. She was our father's younger sister, someone I recalled vaguely from brief visits when my family was living on the road, running from the scores of warrants our father had accumulated in over forty states. In the beginning there had been a kind of giddy joy, a sense of new beginning, a big shiny American Second Chance for my brother and me as she and her naval officer husband initiated adoption proceedings.

Eight months or so after living in government housing projects in Norfolk, Virginia; six months after my father had gotten out of prison; four months after our father had packed my brother and me into a stolen pickup and driven non-stop from Norfolk to San Diego, California, my brother and I were adopted by an aunt and uncle we didn't know, and were living with them and their three young children in Sasebo, Japan.

I have had great difficulty reconciling the decency and sacrifice my ex-stepmother embodies with the meanness of spirit, the petty nature that also defines her. I have had great difficulty untangling the unspeakable affection I feel for someone who saved my life, who gave me a new life, from the loathing I feel for someone who demeaned my brother and me routinely, who abused us verbally and emotionally, for the few years we were under her supervision, and for many years after.

Her shame for her brother, whom she'd adored growing up, was leagues deeper than mine for that man, my father. She instructed me not to tell people I was adopted, and this was partly because of my younger brother's shame, her genuine desire to protect him from our past, but it was her own shame she was tending to most fervently. A truth-teller in every other regard, she built a different past to present to people she met in Sasebo, then Coronado, a past in which she'd been born three years earlier and so had delivered me into the world when she was twenty; a past in which she'd birthed and raised two male children; a past in which the first fourteen years of my life belonged to her.

I'd moved out of her house on my eighteenth birthday. I taught karate and swept, mopped and buffed floors in the geedunk on the Amphib Base. After attending junior college for three semesters, I was taking classes at San Diego State, making vague progress toward a degree in English literature. I'd already lived with a woman disastrously, was in a second disastrous relationship and, between melodramatic breakups and reconciliations with my girlfriend, returned to my adoptive mother's house from time to time to cadge meals.

"Hi, Mom? You here?" I said after climbing the stairs. The downstairs door had been open, the screen door unlocked.

She was lying on her impeccable bed, clothed, leafing through a magazine. I asked her what was for dinner, grinning as she looked up at me over her glasses to say with a glance that of course I could eat with her, Dad and the girls, and of course she did not approve of any aspect of my life. We chatted as she continued to leaf through the magazine, her feet crossed at the ankles, her back propped against the big middle-class headboard of her king-size bed. I chirped something about a course I was taking, and about how things were going at work, and about a student loan I was applying for, and about how I was doing okay with money, and about my girlfriend's mother's hairdressing business, and about Nixon being a prick, which she flicked daggers at me for saying before settling her bored gaze back onto the fashion magazine, and then she said, "Oh yeah, Joan died."

I stared beyond her, trying to figure out what I should feel, but, licking a thumb and turning a page, without even looking up, she added, "Don't act like you're deeply hurt."

I turned and walked down the carpeted steps, her massive silence, her victory over my heart, my loss, at my back.

I put on my gee, yanking tight the ends of the black belt on which my name and rank were stitched vertically in reddish-gold kanji I couldn't read. I was pissed at myself for not feeling anything, and pissed at her for knowing I wouldn't. She'd been fond of Joan. She'd told stories of how as girls, before and right after Joan had married Dick, the two "girls," Joan, nineteen, and she, seventeen, would "play" with their makeup. Joan, she said, had a great sense of humor, laughed all the time, and they were great friends. She even babysat me when I was an infant so Joan and Dick could go out.

Joan had started dying of multiple sclerosis the year before Dick got out of prison. The afternoon Dick packed my brother and me up and sped away, she'd stared off through tears that were about much more than our departure; she was the only person I've ever known who was intimate with her own doom. She'd sat with her aluminum crutches in her lap, silent, tears coursing down her face, my three youngest siblings huddled and whimpering, hungry, confused as always.

In Sasebo, I'd had sixty tournament fights and won forty-nine of them. Most of the wins had been against chumps, though a few were against more or less legitimate opponents. But I was really good at breaking things with my hand, and doing the kata, the stylized dances. I loved doing the dances, in fact. I loved how dignified a body looked doing them well.

I walked in my gee to the alley leading to the backyard of a sailor I was giving private lessons to. He'd installed a makiwara board, and I'd spend hours in his backyard doing kata and beating the board, a six-foot-long two-by-four sunk two feet into the hardpan and reinforced with cement; it was wrapped at the top with coarse rope. When I couldn't make my rent I'd crash in his garage and give private lessons in his backyard, and for the duration of my stay didn't charge him for lessons.

I beat the board for an hour, with both hands; I beat it until my calluses peeled back and I bled, and I kept on beating it. Blood smeared the rope and splattered the wood and I kept beating it. I beat it until I felt something.

Then I stopped and sat in the grass and tried to figure out what I felt. I hated my stepmother. I hated her for smearing my face in Joan's death, and for knowing me so well, and for being a truth-teller who lived a lie because of her shame for my life, where it started and how it got to hers. I hated her for not letting me be a phony, or at least not letting me be one around her. I hated her for my cowardice, my not seeking Joan out before she died. I hated her for her utter lack of sentimentality, for her strength of character, in fact. I hated her for not taking shit from anyone. But I also hated her for her narrow mind and mean spirit, her hatred of anything that threatened her sense of How Things Should Be. I hated her racism and xenophobia. I hated that I called her "Mother," and my mother "Joan." I hated that she hated everything about my life, disapproved of everything, and felt that her own children's lives would have been better off if she'd not adopted my brother and me. I hated her for the pain I caused her by being myself. I hated her for thinking Nixon got a raw deal. But I especially hated her because I desperately desired her approval.

In the kumate, or stylized fights—"kata for two" we Americans sometimes called them—as opposed to in free-style sparring, two people face one another and perform a series of offense/defense dances, switching roles of offender and defender after each series. At some public exhibitions in recent years, elaborately silly staged fights in which the "grand master" takes on a dozen of his acolytes have been nothing more than bad entertainment, not even as authentic as professional wrestling. The kumate, real ones, are pure in their formality, utterly lacking in exhibitionist pretensions. They're not for an audience; they're for the principles. They're a private dance, really.

When my sailor/student/sometimes-landlord came home, he saw me from his kitchen window, and put on his gee and came out. Then he saw my hands, the blood on the makiwara board. He was impressed. My stock went up with him, and it was already ridiculously high. He wanted to beat the board himself. He wanted to pound it until his hands were bloody like mine. He wanted his blood to be joined with mine between the coarse fibers of the rope, on the weathered grain of the wood. He was an idiot, more than a decade older than I, yet prone to the kinds of male fantasies only boys have. I exploited his idiocy, his inflated sense of my prowess.

But I also gave him sound, legitimate instruction. I told him no, he shouldn't beat the board at all. And no, we wouldn't freestyle spar, and no, we wouldn't learn a new kata or work on one he already knew. We would do kumate.

He was half a foot shorter than I, and during classes I'd pair him with another short guy because the kumate look silly when the "combatants" are too different in height. I taught him the one that has five steps, four knife-hand blocks at different angles, then an evasion and take-down followed by a "death blow." We killed each other again and again until he got it right.

MELVIN'S MARVELOUS OLDIES
SUMMER, 1974

Every male between the ages of sixteen and twenty-five, who wasn't a sailor, worked for Joey's Pizza, if only for a week or a day, if only for as long as it took to be on the first trip with a stack of pizzas to the Enterprise, and to forget to set the brake, and so then to have to watch as the Joey's veedub, customized with the "hotbox" where the passenger's seat had been, rolled off the quay wall into San Diego Bay.

That didn't happen to me. I actually don't know whom it had happened to, but Melvin said it happened once, so I'd better set my fucking brake, especially when I'm delivering stacks of pizzas to the Enterprise.

He was chubby late twenties, long red hair and beard, and he ran Joey's kitchen, taking all the calls and directing both the pizza preparation and the fleet of white veedubs that delivered them. Then he directed the cleanup, the prep, and did the bookkeeping. Joey loved him and paid him equal to that love, so Melvin was bucks up, and since he didn't do drugs except a little pot and not much of that, he'd saved a lot of money. He was married to someone whose hair was redder than his, a pretty pale-white Earth Mother with flowing flame and a galaxy of faint freckles. They wanted to have kids but Melvin shot blanks, so they loved a cat preternaturally. I enjoyed visiting them, drinking a little beer and chatting. Melvin's wife, Karen, was quite bright and liked to read; we talked about books because Melvin bragged he'd never read one in his life. His wife had read enough for both of them, he said, and he was glad she now had someone to talk to who'd also read a lot of books.

Melvin was a kind of genius, a man of average intelligence but with a vision of the future. It's as though he'd peeked from 1974 into 1999 or so, had glimpsed guys standing in front of consoles messing with records, music and noise blasting out of monster speakers. It's as though he'd peeked at DJ's of the future but hadn't gotten a good enough look or listen to know what was really going on. He had, however, seen those huge speakers, and guys called DJ's being stars, hundreds of people dancing to the noise they controlled.

So Melvin spent a fair chunk of the money Joey loved him with on massive speakers and two sturdy turntables. He created a huge portable console that he transported in a Chevy van, and already had the finest collection of "oldie" 45s anyone had ever seen. He then tried to get gigs. He'd argue that whomever he was trying to sell himself to should not hire a shitty live band that would only cover its own shitty songs and a little Jethro Tull and maybe Cream, probably some Stones and Ten

Years After but that was it. No, they should hire him to set up his huge black rig on their stage and blast the best oldies through his bitchin' woofers. He argued that he could put on a better show, that people would get up and dance, shout requests, and he had everything, everything, thousands of 45s.

I laughed at him, affectionately. Everyone laughed at him affectionately. Even Karen laughed. But he started getting gigs, and people did get up and dance to "Wooly Bully" and other vintage nonsense, and they wrote requests on napkins and passed them to him while they danced. He called himself a "DJ for private parties instead of on the radio," said that the idea would catch on for private DJ's who worked rooms of people and not over the radio. He was probably the first of that kind. Melvin's Magnificent Oldies. He was the star, master of the music.

But he didn't get enough gigs to justify quitting Joey's, and the ones he got didn't pay him what they'd have paid a live band, and that was primarily why he got them. So he told me to set my fucking brake so the veedub wouldn't roll off the quay wall into San Diego Bay.

Melvin was good to me. He was fair to all the drivers, but he tried to get me the best runs when he could, four or five big orders close together, usually to swabs I could rip off with impunity, because everyone ripped them off. It was a rule: ripping off swabs was okay; ripping off locals was not.

There were fancy ways of ripping them off, methods that required much stealth and preparation, methods that required talent and skill of the sort Barney had in abundance and some of the other drivers exhibited to lesser degrees. But I was not clever that way; I didn't enjoy the process of scamming the way Barney did. So I just brazenly shortchanged them. Before I got out of the car I'd tear off the receipt that was stapled to the top box, hand the three or four boxes to the stoned swab and tell him the receipt had come off by accident, but that he owed me seven or eight bucks more than he actually did; then I'd act hurt if he didn't tip me fifteen percent. I'd do that to every big swabby order except to those going to UDTs and SEALs. They were pretty good tippers, and besides, you just didn't want to rip those guys off.

No swab ever complained; or if he mumbled something about Joey's drivers always ripping him off I'd act indignant and say my father was a naval officer and I loved the Navy. That usually cracked him up long enough for me to get away. And the swabs knew better than to complain to Melvin. Joey's was the only after-hours fast-food delivery service available to them; and the pizzas were superb, and some of the guys also delivered dope, and of course ripped the swabbies off for that, too.

I preferred delivering to the barracks rather than to the aircraft carriers. Melvin didn't screw up much, but he always screwed up which of the stairs we were supposed to go to, and it was a long haul from the car to the stairs and up to the deck, where you usually had to wait for the swab to crawl from the viscera of the great steel beast, and of course he wouldn't be stoned so you couldn't brazenly shortchange him as much as you could the guys in the barracks, who were eternally trashed.

The deliveries to locals were different. Sailors came and went. The locals only died, and not very briskly. It was once calculated that more alcohol was purchased and consumed per capita on Coronado Island than in any other square mile of residential population on the planet. Tenth Street Liquor did a phenomenal delivery business; Retired Vice Admiral I Can't Believe We Lost the Fucking War's brand spanking new widow wouldn't miss a beat: her order for three gallons of Beefeaters every Friday was permanent, and was meant somehow to continue even after her own demise as a kind of testimony to Comfortable Grief.

When we found out someone was ripping off locals we'd gang up on him. We wouldn't smack him around, just shame him. Phil was always getting caught ripping off locals, and we were therefore always shaming him, which was very difficult because Phil was, in almost every sense, unshamable, partly because he was very stupid, partly because he was just gifted that way.

Melvin finally had to take Phil off of local runs entirely when the sixty-year-old son of an ancient mother actually came down to Joey's from Balboa Ave to accuse Phil of taking advantage of the wealthy woman's obvious and legendary dementia, somehow persuading her that a sandwich and coleslaw, not including the tip, cost two hundred and forty-seven dollars.

Melvin's Magnificent Oldies Show got too big for Melvin to handle by himself. He needed roadies, as he called us when we volunteered to help him on nights off from Joey's. We helped him haul the stuff from the van and set it up, and then, when things got started, collected the pieces of napkin and paper with requests scrawled on them, digging through the dozens of little drawers to find each request and stack it in the order it was received. After a record was finished, we put it back in its proper place in its proper drawer. Of course the alphabetical order was enormously screwed up, and Melvin inexplicably filed the 45s as though their titles were proper names, so that "Young Love" was filed as "Love, Young," as though Mr. Love's first name were Young, and Mr. Boardwalk's first and middle names were Under The. But somehow we muddled through, and Melvin got us good and drunk after the show.

Melvin considered the Officer's Club on North Island a prime gig, partly because Special Services paid him very well, but also because the young officers who attended his shows with their wives and dates really appreciated the music. I told Melvin that the place gave me the creeps, that young officers especially gave me the creeps, but that I'd be his roadie for the gig because I owed him. Phil was the only other guy who volunteered, and I flat out told Melvin with Phil standing there that I didn't think it would be a good idea to bring Phil, that he would have a hard time with the filing system, that he would get confused and just be in the way. What I didn't opine out loud was that Phil would probably steal something, silver or liquor, and get caught doing so.

But instead of declining Phil's offer, Melvin just told me to keep an eye on him, that part of my job would be to keep an eye on Phil.

I knew the base quite well, having delivered pizzas to every part of it that wasn't restricted, which was much more of it than wouldn't be now. The Officer's Club was on a hill, a slight rise not far from the main airstrip, and had not looked stylish since about 1952, but had probably seemed quite stylish then. The bars were always packed, I thought, and was probably more or less correct, because to have a successful career as a naval officer required that one drink a lot with other officers. Mostly young officers, which is to say few over thirty-five and the rank of lieutenant commander, attended Melvin's Marvelous Oldies show. There was a churlishness to their frivolity because most of them had entered the service of an undefeated nation, and now found themselves losers.

And they acted like losers; that is, they had the swagger of losers who couldn't admit defeat. They especially danced like losers, and Phil wouldn't stop laughing at them, even pointing at one guy who did something that looked like the Jerk with a little Mashed Potato thrown in, but whose composite effect was that of a massive seizure that would not end in merciful death, but just kept going. Phil said he looked like he was holding on to the end of a downed cable, and it was the only clever thing I'd ever hear Phil say. But I had to yell at Phil over the music not to point, that the guy had seen him pointing and laughing and was now giving us both Fuck You glances, though he didn't miss a lurch in doing so.

Melvin had his headphones on and was absorbed in his work, didn't notice Phil cracking up and pointing, or me trying to make Phil stop, or the guy shooting Fuck Yous at both of us. The guy's partner was barely moving, doing some sort of little hand-jive shuffle with her head down, her face curtained off by her long black hair. It was as though she'd have rather been anywhere but on that dance floor paired with that spastic loser who obviously thought he was as cool as a pimp.

Melvin, ever the pro, segued seamlessly into something slow and clingy by the Righteous Brothers or Marvin Gay, and the guy reached for his partner to press her to him, but she stepped back, turned and walked toward the bar.

This was too much for Phil. He howled so loudly he could be heard over the music, and even Melvin took off his headphones and swiveled his face toward us. The guy strutted up to us, got in our faces and asked us what our fucking problem was, and what drugs we'd been taking, and asked us finally how we'd like our surfboards shoved up our hippie asses.

It was 1974; nobody said "hippie" anymore, except as a joke, but this guy wasn't joking. All three of us had long hair, but then so did just about everybody under thirty who wasn't a sailor, and this guy was maybe twenty-five, had probably just made jg. He'd probably been in ROTC somewhere in Texas from the sound of his accent, maybe SMU, when most of his fellow students had been protesting against the war, even at SMU. They'd probably hated him, and he them, and now he was in our faces calling us hippies, two guys who were too young to be hippies, who were two or three years too young to have had that as a choice of identity.

Phil couldn't keep a straight face. And then I couldn't keep one. This guy calling us hippies was just too much. And all Melvin could think to do was put on another fast song and really crank it up, and all Phil and I could think to do was dance, just like that guy. We started doing a kind of Jerk with a little Mashed Potato thrown in, and we did it for keeps.

THE TRAIN
SUMMER, 1973

You passed through a tiny shop cluttered with stuff that, with the exception of several finely crafted pieces of wooden furniture, people buy for one another knowing it'll get tucked away and forgotten within hours of the formal act of gifting. It was the kind of stuff a nineteen-year-old male felt a little dizzy around, if only because it seemed the official knick knacks of slightly mysterious, and alluring, older females: macramé plant holders, scented candles, soaps with exotic names.

The rear wall was oblique glass, and the Coronado Tea Garden, a charming fenced deck shielded from the sky by a copious catalpa, seemed dreamy from the shop, especially in the afternoon when light slanted from the street and strong shadow bellowed from the roots of the tree.

The Tea Garden had seven tables, but had not found a constituency so they were often empty, which was fine with me. I'd sit and drink coffee and read for hours, sometimes stoned, sometimes not. I usually couldn't afford the sandwiches, which were snooty—lots of bean sprouts and avocado on kinds of bread you couldn't buy in the A&P—by my reckoning, but awfully good. I'd always take the kinds of books to read in the Tea Garden that otherwise put me to sleep, philosophy and social theory and things like that, books I didn't understand but wanted to desperately. It was in the Tea Garden I first read—at least the words on the page—Freud and Marx and their bourgeois acolytes Marcuse and Goodman, Fromm and O. Brown.

The Tea Garden was owned by Tim and his girlfriend Darlene, ten years or so older than I; they'd been hippies for years and stopped, but of course were still a little like that. Tim had long blond hair and so did Darlene, and Tim had the kind of bushy mustache I admired. They were good looking, gentle people, who liked to talk and laugh, and Tim seemed to make enough refurbishing furniture in their backyard on G Avenue to keep the shop and Tea Garden open into the foreseeable future, which turned out to be another eighteen months.

I loved to arrive in the late afternoon at the Tea Garden, books in hand, barefoot as always, and see Tim and Darlene through the oblique glass talking and laughing with their best friends, Peter and Gretchen. They'd always draw me into the conversations, make me feel a part of what was happening. Peter had straight shiny brown hair down to his ass, and was the first man I ever saw who wore an earring. He was getting a lot of money to attend UCSD because he was part Indian. He'd discovered he was part Indian in his sophomore year, and seriously boned up on his tribe and its customs. He also boned up on how to cash in on being an Indian. Peter was in his seventh year at UCSD, and hadn't even begun to exhaust the scholarship opportunities. He'd eventually finish a degree or two in the Humanities, and become a jeweler, amassing a fortune shuttling between San Diego and Cape Town. Gretchen was a tiny woman with fluffy red hair who talked a lot about sex. She admitted to liking it rough, something I wouldn't quite understand for a few years. One time Peter slapped her hard and I jumped up and announced that I was going to kick his ass, which I didn't want to do because I looked up to him, wanted to be like him, but Gretchen was so little and he'd popped her quite hard for joking about his Indianness, calling him Big Chief Circumcised. Gretchen led me away, the side of her face crimson as her hair, an arm around my waist and the other gently holding my arms down, to the shop, and explained, almost in a whisper, stroking my arm as one would a child's, that it was okay for Peter to slap her; he had her permission.

On those occasions I arrived in the late afternoon to the Tea Garden and the two couples were talking and laughing and no one else was there, I felt I was entering upon the kind of world I wanted to occupy, one in which there were hanging plants and knotted wood and sexy catalpa leaves; one in which good coffee flowed and you could go out back and smoke a joint; one in which good looking couples joked endlessly and you could carry around difficult books that contained bits and pieces of the meaning of life.

For a week or so after I'd told Peter I was going to kick his ass for smacking Gretchen, he'd been tepid towards me. He did not doubt I could kick his ass, and nor did I. He knew I had a black belt, that I gave private lessons; he'd heard about the fight I'd had with a big Mexican in the Jack In the Box parking lot in Chula Vista, the other one Chris and I got into in the Greasy Spoon with three sailors. Peter himself was too cool to be a fighter, and knew, besides, how much I admired him, how much I wanted to be too cool to be a fighter, to wear puffy shirts and an earring, hair down to my ass, and be so cool no one would think to call me a faggot.

As I entered the shop the doorbell tinkled, and I saw them through the oblique glass, and heard laughter. They greeted me heartily as I joined them under the ceiling of leaves. I had a little cash from a karate student who'd paid me on time for once, so I ordered one of those fu fu sandwiches with my coffee.

I was a little surprised, and resentful, that another customer occupied the rear table, tucked away in the corner where the wooden wall of the deck met the white plaster of the shop; then noticed who that was reading a thick novel, a muffin and pot of tea before her on the table.

Lorrie Morris had pulled a train at Harry Peck's eight kegger. Scores of guys had lined up to enter her, fidgeting and giggling, punching each other in the arms, before the door of Harry's parents' bedroom. I'd stood in the line for a while, but had felt incredibly stupid doing so, so jumped out, ostensibly to take a piss, but never returned.

I'd heard about trains. Usually they happened when girls passed out from drinking. They were therefore gang rapes, but somehow sanctioned.

No one ever got busted. Lorrie Morris, it was said, had gotten dumped by her boyfriend, whom she'd been engaged to marry. He'd shown up at the kegger with a girl from La Jolla, and Lorrie Morris, the story went, set up a train to get back at her boyfriend.

I found the idea mildly revolting; there was no romance in trains, no kissing, I imagined, and when I pressed a couple of seasoned train riders about what it was like, they confirmed my suspicions; it was mechanical, brutal, messy, stinky, impersonal, and yet they found it exciting, a kind of bonding experience, though of course that's not how they put it. Barney called guys who'd had sex with the same female "squack brothers," and the term was getting around.

I did not wish to be bound in such a way to another guy. And, horror of horrors, I couldn't help imagining what it was like for the girl, lying there, pretty much motionless, being climbed on again and again, the grunting, the rude, shy withdrawals, again and again, the sound of male laughter from the other side of the door.

In the backyard, the beer flowed, the music blasted, and people cavorted. I looked around for a girl to have sex with, saw two I'd had sex with before, but they were into it with other guys, guys I knew, so I kept looking, prowling.

Word was getting around about the train; guys whispering to other guys. One of the guys who was talking to one of the girls I'd had sex with left abruptly to get in line, but another guy I knew got to her before I could.

Two guys were having a punching contest, punching each other in the stomach then guzzling beer; the point seemed to be who would throw up first. Somebody said, "Hey, let Rick punch you!" But neither wanted me in on the game because I really knew how to punch. They stopped and one of them said that instead I should break a brick or a rock. There were girls watching, so I said sure, get me one.

It really had very little to do with karate; it was just a trick. One of the guys brought me a perfect rock, about eight inches long, four wide and three thick, not granite but something with eminent cleavage. You held one end of the thing on your left hand and let the other end rest on a hard surface. The trick, first, was being willing to hit something as hard as you were able with the side of your hand and, second, to time it such that just before impact you lifted the part touching the cement, ever so slightly, so it smacked back into the hard surface. Sometimes I'd have to strike one several times, but such rocks always broke, and even if someone saw the end of the rock lift just before impact, it still looked impressive.

The guys who'd been trying to make each other throw up got a kick out of me smashing that rock. So brought another. And another. Soon there was a circle, and I was smashing rock after rock, just like Lorrie Morris, though I wasn't trying to get back at anyone, except perhaps my father, but I didn't understand that then. I just thought I was making the people around me happy.

She read her book, pinched her muffin and brought it to her mouth without taking her eyes from the print, sipped tea. She was pretty, scrubbed looking, wore the tasteful clothes of the mid-twenties career woman she was, part owner with her mother of a successful clothing store. She looked up and saw me staring at her, smiled.

I smiled back, dipped my chin. She knew, probably vaguely, who I was because her ex-boyfriend used to drop by Dirty Dan's to get high, and brought her along once or twice. I recalled that she'd toked daintily, as though she did it only not to offend anyone.

I was drawn to her out of morbid curiosity, but also because she was pretty and was reading a thick book. I asked her what she was reading. It was *Gone With the Wind*; she said her family was from the South, that she went back often to South Carolina. I sat with her. She chattered about an evil great-great grandfather who'd owned slaves and hanged a few of them, and about how the air smelled after spring rain in Charleston.

Darlene brought my coffee and sandwich, and I found myself in a kind of dating situation with Lorrie Morris, who in one night had been entered by a fair percentage of the non-military affiliated males on Coronado Island, for word really got around, and the line stayed long for hours, into dawn, as guys lined up for seconds and thirds, and guys called other guys on the phone to come over and get in on the action.

I'd given up breaking rocks long before Lorrie did. And had glanced at the line as dawn swelled upon the high overcast that would burn off by noon, and stumbled off toward my '67 Mercury station wagon, alone and a little drunk, a little stoned.

Did she know I knew? She seemed a happy person. Perky, even. She asked about the book I'd brought in, and I mumbled a little about the Frankfurt School, knowing absolutely nothing substantial of what I was holding forth about, but she seemed interested, impressed, even. After about an hour, our conversation began to blend with the one Tim and Darlene, Peter and Gretchen, were having. It got dark and Tim turned the lights on, one yellow light and tiny white Christmas lights that ran in rows along the dark wood of the walls, and around the trunk of the catalpa. The Tea Garden was even more beautiful at night, and one could smell the high tide just two blocks away, and there was a little wind, and a fine chill.

Lorrie had never met those people, and liked them a lot, and they liked her. And I realized I was part of a couple, with Lorrie, as far as Tim and Darlene, Peter and Gretchen, were concerned.

Darlene locked up the shop, and Peter made a quick run to Central Liquor. I had about a quarter ounce of weed in my back pocket. Tim got some papers from the kitchen.

What followed was the sort of fellowship in which I am no longer capable of participating. We drank several bottles of the cheapest red, and smoked joints I rolled so poorly it was a running joke among my several sets of friends. Lorrie toked daintily, and drank her share, and began to glow.

Tim turned up the classical music that was always playing low in the Coronado Tea Garden, but not enough to inhibit conversation. Peter told a long story about visiting relatives on a reservation in New Mexico, pulled two turquoise stones from a brown pouch around his neck and passed them around. He said that "his people" had given them to him to ward off evil spirits, and Gretchen chimed in that he'd bought them in a reservation gift shop; Peter, with mock haughtiness, replied, "Yeah, but my people owned that goddamned store!" and everybody cracked up.

Lorrie asked Peter if he was "full-blooded," and Gretchen guffawed heartily. "He's a Polish Jew!" she exclaimed. "His daddy knocked up an Irish Catholic whose mother, it turns out, was half Indian. So Tonto here's been working a scholarship scam. The problem is he believes his own bullshit." Tim, Darlene and I chuckled a little, though everyone but Lorrie expected Gretchen to catch one in the chops. But after doing five seconds of hard-ass staring, Peter chuckled, too.

My friends, closer to Lorrie's age than I, started asking her questions, discovering little connections, who knew whom, who graduated when. Everyone knew Andy Morrison, Jim Morrison's brother who stayed in Coronado, and the Morrison sister whose name no one could remember, though Peter knew she was married to a Brit who fancied himself a poet. Everyone also knew, it turned out, Lorrie's ex-boyfriend's older sister; she and Gretchen had gone to UC Santa Cruz at the same time; both had majored in Psych.

"Lynda liked to take it in the ass," Gretchen said rather thoughtfully.

"I beg your pardon," Lorrie said.

"She liked it vaginally, but she liked a big guy also to plug her in the ol' bung."

"We weren't very close," Lorrie said, staring down.

"Don't mind her," Peter chimed, "she's a nympho. It's all she thinks about." There was nervous chuckling. Everyone was a little drunk, a little stoned, but my friends could feel Lorrie's unease.

"Hay, I'm sorry, kid," Gretchen said. "How long did you date him?"

"Four years. We were going to be married." We watched the tears well up, glisten and sparkle in the aggregate shine of tiny lights.

"What happened?" Darlene asked.

"Let's take a walk," I said, and took Lorrie's hand. "I'll see you guys later."

So now she knew I knew. But she let me hold her hand. We were quiet. She took off her shoes to walk on the beach. We walked the waterline from the Hotel Del Coronado toward the fence of North Island Naval Air Station.

After almost half an hour of quiet, of walking slowly and holding hands, she said, "Most of them couldn't even do it."

I didn't say anything.

"They just wanted the others to think they were doing it."

"Most?"

"I don't know. Maybe not. But a lot. More than a few."

"So what'd you do with those?"

"Talked a little. Promised I wouldn't tell anyone they couldn't do it."

"Why do you think some of them couldn't do it?" I really wanted to know, because I'd probably have been one of them.

"Because they were scared of how I was doing it. Some were probably scared they wouldn't measure up."

"Maybe they were just decent," I suggested.

"The decent ones never came through the door," she said.

There were fires farther up the beach, couples on blankets. Dogs lay in the sand by the fires. Some folks were playing volleyball, getting a kick out of the fact that it was too dark to see the ball. A jet squealed off the northern-most runway of the air base. I thought about that line, how the guys kept queuing up, how much fun they seemed to have just standing in that line, the wise cracking, the hoots and hollers that met every guy who emerged from the dark of that room, and accompanied each one into it.

Deep Fried
Summer, 1974

Neither of us belonged there, at least by our own reckoning. Mickey Rutter was the oldest of eight children; his mother was pretty and didn't look like she'd had eight children, but I didn't make the connection between multiple childbearing and aesthetic degradation, so I wasn't impressed; I just thought she was hot, and Mickey's father was some weird form of warrant officer, a sailor caught in that military zone between noncom and officer, but quite high up as warrants go. They actually lived in Officers' Housing on the Amphibious Base, in a squat standard-issue brick house which was too small for them, and which lay at the beginning of the Silver Strand highway down to Imperial Beach and all things Mexican. They otherwise never could have afforded to live in Coronado, where neither Mickey nor I thought we belonged.

Mickey moved out of his family's house while he was still in high school. He got along with his parents and siblings, but everyone needed more room, and Mickey was getting tired of having sex with his girlfriend on the beach, in fields and in his '64 Volkswagen. I moved out of my stepparents' house because my aunt/stepmother was mean, and because my uncle/stepfather was depressed about losing the war in Vietnam, which he seemed to think he'd botched single-handedly. My stepfather was a lieutenant commander, and Mickey was the only guy I knew in Coronado whom I outranked according to the unwritten, and largely unspoken, rule of shadow rank each military dependent observed, even after one was no longer legally a dependent, as was true for Mickey and me once we'd moved out of our families' houses.

Mickey and I worked at the geedunk on the Amphibious Base; he was a jack-of-all kind of guy, and sometimes worked the line, in particular the grill; sometimes the cash register, the less busy of the two because he'd get frustrated with the sailors and marines hassling him to ring up quicker. Sometimes he'd bus tables and even help me do the floors.

All the thirtyish women who worked the line, black and white, loved Mickey, flirted with him constantly and he flirted back, knew just what to say to such women, which always seemed something entirely goofy and not at all what I would have said. But they always cracked up, joked about wanting to take him home. They were always calling him "cute," and he clearly liked their calling him that. I was cute, too, I was fairly sure, but none of those women ever publicly announced that I was. I didn't care, not much anyway. Mickey was obviously more their type, perhaps because it seemed a certainty that when he was thirtyish he'd be working at precisely the sort of job he and they now worked, only by then he'd be some kind of manager. They probably figured I'd be dead or in jail by then, or in a completely different line of work, one requiring dogged persistence but little charm.

Our boss was Esther Hale, who was six feet tall and weighed maybe a hundred and ten pounds. She'd started working at the geedunk "way before the War," and we assumed she meant the Second World War, but weren't entirely certain, given that she was older than rain. Her arms and legs were covered with the bruises of an active old age, and her hair, short and perfect, was as white as her uniform. She shamed us daily by getting on her knees or standing on a chair to inspect one of the dozens of corners that seemed to appear and disappear in that odd building, like in those Escher posters folks used to like to stare at stoned. She'd get sad gazing into a filthy corner and then quietly go back to the pantry and bring out an aluminum pot filled with scalding water, put on yellow rubber gloves and start scraping at the crud with Ajax and steel wool. Mickey and I would stand there helpless while she scrubbed, getting looks from whoever was around, the retarded dishwasher Herman, or a last customer, a seaman second-class just finished with his fried slop and adjusting his silly white hat to leave. We'd stand there, then try to talk to her, apologize for missing that corner; at those moments we'd do anything, seeing that old woman, so close to death, scrubbing crud, anything for her, and we'd tell her so. But she'd just sigh, scrub and say, finally, that all she wanted was for us to take our jobs seriously.

Mickey and I loved Esther Hale as one loves a force of nature, as when one says, "I love the snow," or "I love a summer storm," though it was her preternatural consistency that awed us, so to love her was to love as one may a sunrise or sunset, or a phase of the moon.

She arrived at 5 a.m. exactly, and left at 6 p.m. exactly, six days a week. She managed every aspect of that cafeteria, from purchasing and hiring and the books, to monitoring cruddy corners. She knew exactly how many forks, how many knives, spoons, pots, hamburger patties, tins of lard, there were, because she'd counted, counted everything. Mickey said he'd once come upon her in her office counting staples.

The place did a phenomenal business for one obvious reason: It was the only place to eat besides the mess. So hundreds of guys, almost all enlisted, came each day for what you couldn't have in the mess, which is to say some kind of choice, though what one chose was most likely to be fried.

And it was that one task Mickey and I loathed more than any other: emptying the deep fryers and reloading them with lard, then getting down on our stomachs and cleaning the wretched space beneath, which was always caked with a swamp of organic matter, including the legs-up corpses of roaches we assumed died in a kind of ecstasy there. It was a one-man job, and one of us had to do it each week and endure Esther Hale's inspection, the old woman putting down a white towel and spreading flat out on her stomach with her little flashlight in her teeth, insisting, after a solid minute of gazing and touching, that the tiles there were still too slick, still had a film of grease on them, and our despair was bottomless because it was impossible to clean that area so that there was, forensically speaking, absolutely no grease on the tiles. But we tried and tried, and disappointed Esther Hale again and again, though she never stopped being kind to us, giving me rides into town to save me the long walk after work, loaning Mickey money he never had to pay back.

Mickey got called a swab a lot, which in the youth culture of early Seventies Coronado was far worse than being called a motherfucker, and he did indeed act like a certain kind of sailor, that is, the kind who didn't mind being one. He said the beach was only good at night and then only for screwing, and he didn't smoke dope unless he had to, that is, unless not doing so would require more explanation than it was worth. He'd usually smoke one time around anyone he met so at least that person wouldn't think he was a narc, which was the only thing, besides a cop, worse than a swab.

Mickey loved sex at least as much as I did, but only did it with one girl; he'd found a girlfriend quickly when he arrived in Coronado, one who got called swab bait even before she hooked up with him. They were inseparable, one of those couples always tied up with one another, French kissing indiscriminately in public, always glowing from some form of recent sex. In fact, Mickey was the most faithful guy in all of Coronado, certainly more faithful than I, for I was a kind of slut, sleeping around a lot and with little discrimination; he only made it with one girl other than his girlfriend the whole time I knew him, and it happened when he and that second girl were drunk and she came on to him with an irresistible intensity. I was there; I saw it. His girlfriend, alas, was out of town on a family trip; I brought two girls to Mickey's apartment for beers, without even asking him, and the one who wasn't with me pretty much rode Mickey like a stick pony right into motherhood.

When Mickey found out the girl was pregnant, he did what to his mind was the only decent thing: he offered to pay for half the abortion, and seemed baffled that she did not find his offer reasonable. He was stunned when the girl's mother informed him in one brisk phone call to the geedunk that the girl was sixteen and indeed planned to have the baby. Her father, a rear admiral under whom, as it turned out, Mickey's father served, still had to be informed of the "situation," but the girl, who did look old for her age, and her mother were certain that Daddy, a devout Roman Catholic whose only philosophical divergence from Church doctrine was over the death penalty (and early indications were that he would have it applied to a broad range of crimes, including statutory rape), would want her to keep the baby.

Of the two of us, I deserved much more to be in the situation Mickey was in; but it was in fact he, and not I, who was in it, and though I felt scummy for being at least a little responsible for the turn toward doom his life had taken, I also couldn't help feeling a tiny bit exhilarated that it was he and not I careening toward the gooey dark of utter uncertainty, no doubt a wretched place of filthy grease and dead roaches.

In the karate dances, one confronted overwhelming attacks by multiple belligerents with an even more overwhelming dignity indicated primarily by posture and precise movement. I'd tried to teach Mickey some of the elementary kata; he'd attended a few lessons with a group of four guys who'd been studying with me twice a week for most of a year. My problem as a karate teacher was that I couldn't take guys' money once I'd gotten to know them, so I was teaching those four pretty much for free, and they were getting damned good, especially one of them who just happened to be a natural athlete. They were serious, and couldn't tolerate Mickey not being serious, so they asked me not to invite him back. He'd crack up at my assuming the authority of a teacher. That was his main problem; he couldn't take me seriously and found it incredible that everyone else did. He marveled at my transformation as I donned my gee and tied my black belt, already a little frayed from use, marveled and found it ridiculous.

I had no problem with Mickey finding my transformation ridiculous; I knew I was ridiculous, and yet I had a kind of faith in the kata. When Mickey argued that all that fancy movement wouldn't get anyone out of a pickle at the Long Bar in Tijuana, I agreed, but then explained that the real point of the kata was not movements one should perform precisely if attacked, because the movements were only the ideal. The secret was not the complex combinations of movement, but the attitude with which one performed them. If you couldn't climb inside the attitude it didn't matter how well you performed the movements, and if you climbed inside the attitude and didn't perform precisely you were simply an idiot. You had to pull the movements together with the attitude.

Mickey would put up with such talk for about four minutes. He understood, in the abstract, that the kata were how you learned the right way to do offensive and defensive movements in combination, and that only then you learned to do freestyle sparring, which comes closest to how fights really go down. He wanted me just to teach him how to freestyle spar because of its obvious practical application, and I explained, emphatically, that you just couldn't do it that way. You could only freestyle after you'd gotten through the Peons, one through five; you had to do them perfectly before you could learn to fight, even though one didn't use any of the movements in freestyle. Why? Because, goddamnit, that's the way I was taught by Yasuzato-san, a ninth-degree black belt, a seventy-year-old man who could tear the asshole out of a rabid water buffalo.

He knew I could fight; he'd sat stunned at two in the morning as Chris Papasovis and I took on three sailors who where looking for trouble in the Nite & Day, of all places, busted them up quite quickly and efficiently. He just thought that that dignity I suddenly assumed when teaching and doing karate was utterly false, because otherwise I wouldn't be such a goof at work and when we hung out. If it were real, that dignity, I wouldn't turn it off, wouldn't want to. If it were real I'd move through the world like a prince, not a scumbag.

Of course, he had a point. But what I couldn't get across was that it was something you entered, not something that entered and inhabited you.

Mickey needed to go to Presidio Park. He was distraught, and bought two six-packs of sixteen-ounce Buds and told me I had to come with him so he wouldn't drink both and get in a wreck driving back to Coronado.

Mickey and I would drive once a week in his bug to Presidio to sit and drink beer and talk, overlooking the lights of San Diego. It was the only time he wasn't working or hanging on his girlfriend, whom I quite liked. We talked mostly about how we didn't belong in Coronado, and what we'd do to get out eventually. I was on a two-year plan. But Mickey figured he could no longer afford a long-term exit strategy. He figured rear admiral Daddy was going to destroy his own father's career, and thereby the equanimity of Mickey's entire family, in short order, and find some way to reactivate the California gas chamber just for Mickey Rutter.

As we sat and slugged back the tepid beers, we both agreed that Mickey had to get out of town, way out. He had a grandmother, his mother's stepmother, in Tucson, who was crazy about him and would let him stay there while he looked around for a job. He was pretty sure his bug would make it to Tucson. He just needed some money. He had thirty-seven bucks stashed away, but needed more. Did I have some I could loan him?

I was very fond of Mickey, and had over eight hundred dollars saved, but I wasn't giving any of my Two-Year Plan money to Mickey Rutter, even though I admitted that I was partially responsible for his dire circumstances. I told him he should ask Esther for the money; she'd front him three or four hundred for sure. She was rich because she hadn't spent any of her government paychecks since Eisenhower, Millie the PX bookkeeper had once asserted. All Esther Hale did was work and stash away her money. And she'd never balked at loaning Mickey small amounts, and never reminded him about his debts. The only problem was that three or four hundred would require some sort of explanation.

Neither of us had ever lied to Esther Hale; it had simply never occurred to us to do so. We'd lie to anyone else, especially each other, and did so often. But we'd never thought to lie to Esther, even when doing so would have made our lives at work easier. She'd ask me if I'd remembered to clean the mop and bucket before putting them away, and I'd tell her I'd sprayed out the bucket but had simply rinsed and squeezed out the mop and hung it on its peg. I would then of course have to go back into the scullery and clean the mop with soap and hot water, squeeze it out and hang it again on its peg, and then clean up the mess that had resulted from cleaning the mop. She'd ask Mickey if he'd scraped down the grill with the pumice before turning off the gas, and he'd say no, but he'd scraped it off really thoroughly with the spatula, and wiped it down with rags; and of course he'd then have to fire it back up, pour fresh grease over it, and press and slide that black stone into the metal of the grill in hundreds of small circles.

"So what are you going to tell her?" I asked, burped, swigged, and tossed the can in the backseat.

"What do you mean what am I going to tell her?"

"I mean, like, you're not going to tell her you knocked up a two-star admiral's infant daughter, are you?" I popped another tab.

"Why would I put it like that?"

" You mean, you're going to walk in there and say, Esther, I need four hundred dollars to get out of town because I got Admiral Daddy's sixteen-year-old daughter in the family way?"

"What's family way?"

When we were stumped we'd ask each other questions like that instead of having a real conversation; it was how we kept the words flowing until one of us, through the beer haze, could muster something at least resembling a thought. Finally, one formed, it seemed, in both our heads at once.

"Don't tell her anything," I mumbled.

"She knows I wouldn't ask if I didn't really need it," Mickey mumbled.

"She won't even ask you anything. She'll just give it to you," I said more resolutely.

"We can stay up all night and drive over to the geedunk and catch her at five," Mickey said.

"We'll look like shit," I chirped. "If we show up at five and you tell her you've got to go to Tucson pronto, us looking like shit and all, she'll know it's important and won't ask any questions. She'll just give you the cash."

It was thus we persuaded each other that Mickey wouldn't have to lie to Esther Hale, that she would fork over four hundred greenback dollars to a nineteen-year-old utility-infielder geedunk employee, the son of a warrant officer, a sweet and decent guy as sharp as a doorknob but oozing charm. As it turned out, it wasn't that we couldn't lie to Esther Hale, but that we were simply unable to do so successfully.

"You're lying," she said flatly. I was sitting next to Mickey; we faced her across her desk. She'd asked Mickey why he was going to Tucson, and without missing a beat he'd said his grandmother was dying.

"Tell me the truth, Mickey," she said, and he did.

In several of the kata, there is a particularly beautiful move from a "cat stance"; you jump over the body of someone you have already disabled in order to engage one of the other attackers. It is the ultimate move from defensive to offensive posture, and is very dramatic. As I sat there listening to Mickey spill his life's bile to that ancient woman, that embodiment of constancy, it suddenly occurred to me that for the foreseeable future I could be solely responsible for emptying and cleaning the deep fryer, and cleaning under it, that if this truth-telling were successful, there would be no one, nothing mediating between Esther Hale and me.

Outside, through Esther Hale's window, palm trees swayed in the new light. Military stuff began to grind its portion of a good day down to useable materials. Just minutes ago, it seemed, our country had lost a war, or had been lost in it. But this was a new day. Lessons had been learned. The sky over Coronado was open for business, and no one, not even Mickey Rutter, would miss the formal beauty of it all.

THE UNLUCKY
SUMMER, 1973

Maybe I was checking out his girlfriend, but every other guy in the Long Bar in Tijuana was also checking her out. So why he locked onto me seemed mysterious, except that perhaps I looked like the easiest target, with my girlish hair and my earring that not even rock stars were wearing in 1973.

As he approached I actually smiled and dipped my chin. When he said he was going to kick my ass I was momentarily puzzled. I was with Jimmy and Bink, and the music was loud.

"What he say?" Bink screamed over the music, cupping his hand to my ear.

"He said he's going to kick my ass," I yelled back through a cone I made with my hands. Bink passed this on to Jimmy.

The guy was my height, though much thicker. He looked Mexican but didn't sound Mexican. He was dressed like someone with money but no taste, his shiny black shirt unbuttoned to his solar plexus so that his ample chest hair, in which a gold crucifix nestled, was the black flag of his manliness.

I figured I could take him because he was clearly drunk and I wasn't, and because I was in good shape from my recently intensified karate workouts. The main problem as I saw it was getting tossed into a TJ jail, where I'd get murdered and my corpse defiled by an army of sexually undiscerning banditos. So I tried to laugh him down and buy him off with a drink, but he wouldn't go for it. So I asked him point-blank if he had a knife or a gun on him, and he assured me he didn't; I eyeballed him neck to shoes and concluded that he probably didn't. His girlfriend came over and tried to pull him away, but that only made him more determined to fight me. So I said, "Okay, okay. Where you want to do it?" The music had stopped. My ears rang.

"Right here, motherfucker," he said, and I suggested that we find an alley, some kind of open space where there wouldn't be a lot of people. Bink and Jimmy were trying to figure out what their roles should be. They knew they shouldn't intervene, but also didn't want to desert me; neither did they wish to have their own corpses defiled by banditos.

It was too easy. He tossed haymakers. All I had to do was duck. Then I kicked him in the nuts. My rule was that if the other guy started it, his nuts were in play.

Then I popped him three times on the left side of his head and he went down hard. I immediately felt terrible. Blood was pouring from his nose and his left eye was getting huge and dark even in the dimness of the Long Bar, which had distorting mirrors on the walls like in a funhouse, and I caught a glimpse of myself, stretched and flattened out like a cartoon figure in Silly Putty, gawking at the damage I'd just done to another human being.

Bink suggested that we leave; he and Jimmy grabbed my arms and hustled me out. Everyone in the bar had frozen for a few seconds, even the guy's girlfriend, until we reached the door, and she screamed and one of the bartenders started yelling in Spanish.

On the street we ran like hell. When we got to Jimmy's van I was shaking. Bink and Jimmy were chortling about how I'd clocked the guy, fucked him up but good, but I couldn't bask in their admiration. The guy had been drunker than I'd thought at first; I could have just kept ducking and simply humiliated him, slapped him around and laughed at him. If I'd done that, I might even have walked with his girlfriend. I didn't have to fuck him up. I was shaking and trying to figure out why I'd fucked him up when I'd immediately realized, as soon as he'd started swinging like a huge child who'd never been taught how to punch, I didn't have to.

We rolled toward the border, but then Bink wondered aloud if I'd killed the guy or put him in a coma, and if I had wouldn't the border guards already be watching out for three gringos who looked like us. Then Jimmy suggested that perhaps I should walk across, and they'd meet me on the other side.

They were being cowards, but I didn't blame them, so I got out of the veedub van as it sat two hundred yards back in the line to get into the U.S. I actually preceded them across the border, didn't even get looked at as I crossed, and waited on the sidewalk in front of the Shell station, smoking a cigarette, worrying about that guy.

Something had snapped in me. I'd popped him fast and hard three times after I'd tapped him in the nuts just hard enough to buckle his knees. After I'd tapped him, he'd been helpless. I'd struck a guy who was helpless, drunk and helpless, three times in his face, busted him up just to bust him up. That wasn't self-defense. It certainly wasn't honorable. It was petty and mean, everything karate wasn't supposed to be, what a warrior wasn't supposed to be.

Jimmy and Bink wouldn't stop talking about it, told everyone. And the story got inflated in the telling. By the next day, guys were coming up to me in Coronado saying they'd heard I'd fucked up six guys in Tijuana, and I didn't have the heart or patience to correct them; I'd just turn silent and try to get away.

I watched the news and read the paper to see if anything was reported about the guy dying or being in a coma, but nothing showed up, and after a few days I figured he must have been okay, though the third time I'd struck him I'd felt something give.

I couldn't help imagining the event from his point of view, though it was difficult to imagine being that big and acting that tough and not knowing how to punch. Anybody like that must have had, I figured, a lot of experience getting the shit beaten out of him.

And some people, I was coming to realize, were just like that, born to get their asses whipped repeatedly. They, the unlucky, weren't that different from the rest of us. Some even had long runs of good fortune, which often simply meant they wouldn't get publicly humiliated for many weeks, even months at a stretch. But eventually the sky opened up over them, gushing humiliations. I'd been merely an agent of that guy's chronically ill fortune.

But when I saw a guy stretched out in the sand, just inches above the low-tide waterline, I didn't chalk his situation up to luck or its lack except as mine was being affected. It was dawn; I'd been up all night on mild acid, was coming down with a battery of joints, and didn't need to discover a sailor in his whites stretched out unconscious in the wet sand. I could see he was breathing, so figured I could just keep walking, but the tide was reaching him, soaking his pants, and the guy wasn't moving; would he remain that way and get covered by the rising water? Would that make me feel terrible? Yes, passing that swab and then finding out that he'd drowned would definitely be a bummer.

"Hey, fella," I said, straddling his chest, nudging him with my bare foot. Nothing.

"Hey, guy, better get your ass about ten feet up the beach or you'll be cavorting with the fishes in about twenty minutes," I said, shaking him harder with my foot. His face was red and puffy; the whites of his eyes showed from cracks. I toyed with dragging him about ten feet, and stealing his wallet to pay myself for the service, but immediately felt ashamed for having such a thought. I did, though, figure that I should pull his wallet to find out who he was.

He was from Oregon and had an Irish name, something with an "O" and an apostrophe, and about eighty dollars. I was pissed at him for being so fucked up and putting me in this position of holding eighty bucks I quite deserved for having all but saved his sorry swab life, but couldn't take it, not like that. If he'd ordered pizzas from Joey's on a Friday or Saturday night, the only nights I delivered pies to the naval bases in Joey's veedub bugs, I'd have ripped him off within an inch of human decency. I'd have extorted every penny I could squeeze out of him and his swab buddies, but I couldn't rip him off this way, perhaps because there was no sport to it, perhaps because whenever I found myself in such situations, I'd ask myself what my criminal father would do, and then do the opposite. It was how I kept from hating myself. It was how I remained decent in my own eyes, even if I stared into distorting mirrors. And Dick, I knew, would have taken the money as well as the guy's nice leather wallet, and of course his watch, even though it was a cheap one, and probably would have taken a hard look at the guy's spit-shined, government-issue black shoes.

I took ten bucks because I was hungry and broke, then five more and stuffed the wallet back in his pocket before I could pluck any more bills. Then I slapped the guy pretty hard three times. He started coming around, moaning, then lifted his head and spewed beer and multicolored chunks into the sand, the stench of which made me feel I'd definitely earned the fifteen bucks.

"Gloria," he moaned.

"No, pal, I'm not Gloria," I said. And started to walk away.

"Gloria," he sobbed, and I couldn't leave him. He was weeping and calling Gloria, definitely sick in his heart and mind beyond anything I could recognize, sick in his heart for Gloria, and reeking of what his body had not been able to process of the previous night, a time of pathological self-pity and self-destruction. The guy was obviously a deep feeler; only deep feelers got into such predicaments. I was not a deep feeler, but respected warily those who were. I'd learned to mute almost everything, my despair at my mother's suffering, my feelings of loss for my younger brothers and sister, my feeling of being more alone in the world than anyone I knew. I was not able to feel deeply, or what I felt nestled so far down it might as well have been vaulted, or simply at a depth that sunlight couldn't reach.

He wept convulsively, rolling into a fetal position and pressing his flushed cheek into the mellow stench he'd spewed.

"Come on, buddy," I said as gently as I could. "Can you get up?"

His weeping ratcheted down until he was just sucking and blowing staccato.

"Can you get up?" I asked again.

He looked around, as though for the source of my voice, even though I was crouched right in front of him. His eyes rolled up in his head and he said, "Get away, you piece of shit."

I got angry then hurt. I rose, turned, walked.

But then I stopped. I felt responsible and curious. "Man, why don't you let me help you up. I'll call a cab," I said.

"Why don't I put a foot up your ass, queer."

A fighter jet shrieked over. Surfers were arriving in their black wetsuits, blond, tanned and indifferent to everything but the ocean, its mood their mood.

"Man, you're really fucked up," I half-whispered.
"Not too fucked up to rip your head off and shit down your neck," he rasped.

He was small, and had a squeaky voice. He reminded me of a tiny dog that would strain at its leash and make a racket when an enormous one crossed its path. The way he spoke made me pity him. "Buddy, you couldn't even beat your meat right now. Why don't you let me call a cab?"

He rose, with dramatic effort, to his elbows, then sat up. His head was killing him. Mine was still sparking from the acid, but it didn't hurt. This guy was poisoned. He wished he were dead. And suddenly I realized that indeed he'd tried to kill himself and failed.

"Who's Gloria?" I asked. His face flushed a deeper red and filled with loathing. It took him twenty seconds, but he managed to rise to his feet.

"I'm going to kill you, faggot," he growled.

"Please don't," I said, and meant that I didn't want him to exert any effort coming after me, that I didn't want him to hurt himself any more than he already had.

"You pussy!" he shouted.

"Yeah, man!" I said, "I'm a pussy, man. You got it right, dude. Don't fuck me up, please! But why don't you let me call you a cab, all right? Which base you stationed on?"

He found me disgusting. I wanted to take him down to the water and wash the puke off his face. I knew he'd get in trouble going back to the base looking like that. "Hey, man, why don't you wash your face a little," I said.

"You want to suck my dick, queerbait?" he replied.

"No, I'm sure Gloria does that just fine," I said, and his rage exploded. He stumbled toward me, and I backed away. Each step he took toward me I matched backwards, until he fell on his face. The dry sand stuck to the crust of puke. He had tears in his eyes, pale blue in rosy pools, and he looked up at me and wanted to kill me almost as much as he wanted to crawl into Gloria's lap, as much as he wanted to crawl deep inside her and fall asleep forever.

Nothing was more important to me than making sure that guy didn't destroy himself. And I decided that second to do the unspeakable: I would call the police. "Hey, dude, I'm outta here. You be cool." And I trotted away.

On Ocean Boulevard, I paused to figure out how I'd get to a phone, but I saw a Coronado Police cruiser turn from Star Park, and waved it down.

I was still tripping, a little. And I probably reeked of weed. I told the cop about the swab, that he seemed really fucked up. The cop was clearly annoyed, but was duty-bound to check out my claims.

"Do I know you?" the cop said. He was a meta-cop, so clean-cut he was almost cool.

"I've never caused any trouble," I blurted.

"You're the karate guy," he said. "My little brother's Tim."

"Tim Hogan?" I said. He was one of my students.

"Yeah," he smiled.

"Tim never told me his brother was a cop," I said.

"Would *you*?" he said, and I kind of chuckled. Of course I wouldn't brag about my brother being a cop. It was the worst thing to be. Swabs, narcs, and then cops. I had no idea how the guy had recognized me. Maybe from one of the cheesy posters I'd had made to advertise my classes.

"Anyway, look, that swab's super fucked-up. I think he's, like, suicidal," I said.

The meta-cop called for backup, which arrived in about five minutes. I sat on a bench that was at the height of the border of boulders between Ocean Boulevard and the beach, the sun at my back. I watched the cops peel the guy from the sand and all but carry him toward the steps leading to my perch, and down to the street. He didn't look at me as they led him up the steps and past me. They didn't even look at me. They shoved him in the backup's caged backseat, uncuffed. He lay down on his back and stared at the ceiling as both cruisers hummed slowly away.

I fired up a joint and watched the surfers, tiny in the distance, mount four-footers into the sun. I thought about all the deep feelers I'd known in my life, particularly Louanna, with whom I'd lived for part of a year, my first love, who last I heard was polishing her French with a middle-aged lounge singer, one of those Frenchman who plays acoustic guitar and makes a virtue of singing badly but soulfully. I wondered if Louanna was still trying from time to time to kill herself.

And I thought about a child who'd terrified me when I was a child; a boy younger than I whose brother had been murdered by white guys down at the tracks where we all, black and white, gathered into burlap bags potatoes spilling from penny-colored boxcars that slowed through Elizabeth City, North Carolina. That kid had walked in his sleep naked every morning for an entire spring, screaming his brother's name as he staggered down the street, then returned to his house in the black section of town, screaming that name before waking.

I considered myself extremely lucky not to be a deep feeler, not to be someone who tipped easily into inconsolable despair. I was lucky not to be delicate. I could feel passion, especially passionate anger, but life to me was not a disease; sadness was something that, when I entered it, I could usually feel around inside of and find a hole through which to crawl out fairly quickly.

Doing the kata, the karate dances I so loved, one learned that successful struggle was primarily an issue of posture and equanimity, of split seconds of savagery punctuating calm and measured movement.
But being stoned and, just that moment, physically still, was okay. The ocean and its tiny riders were okay. I had a date lined up and would probably get laid before midnight and that was very good. I was no deep feeler, and I was therefore lucky.

THE COST
SUMMER, 1974

Bronco wore his filthy cowboy hat every waking hour. He didn't take it off indoors, and when he slept he put it down by his feet. Melvin and Darlene had thrown a party the night before for their birthdays that were only three days apart. I'd gone back to my place at around two, but promised I'd come back and help clean up in the late morning.

Several of the folks who'd attended the party were sleeping on the rug under yellow sheets; Bronco, his hat hanging on the big toe of his left foot that was propped on his right, was loudly grinding his breath on the room's stale air, but no one stirred.

His hair was a mess. Kinky and reddish black, it was poofed and twisted in places, uneven all over. He could've had a nice 'fro, gone to a black barber and gotten it taken care of, but instead he wore that hat, sweat-stained, food-stained, oil-stained from working on his van interminably.

The only child of old parents, his father a retired E9, Master Chief Petty Officer, Bronco was the only black guy in Coronado who wasn't a swab. He'd graduated from Coronado High in the early Sixties and joined the tribe of males who'd finished high school but never got off the island, who worked bad jobs in order to spend what was left of their youths in a kind of paradise. They were charmed, but Circe was nowhere to be found, and Odysseus had simply sneaked away without them.

Bronco's best buddy was Warren, who was just like him but white and didn't wear a hat. Everybody thought it was so cool that Warren called Bronco a nigger sometimes, that they were so tight he could use the word. I was certain that, though Bronco grinned when Warren called him one, in his heart he hated being called that name. He just didn't know how to get out of that aspect of their friendship. They were so close their hearts were mysteries to one another, as happens in love.

I didn't like Bronco. I wanted to but just didn't. I'd grown up in black neighborhoods when my father was in prison. I'd been poor on welfare and had middle-class black friends who'd pitied me. In Elizabeth City, our dilapidated house had been the first one occupied by white people; that is, in the early Sixties we'd occupied the border of the black section of a small southern town noted for its hyperactive KKK. On the navy base in Sasebo, and on the ones on Coronado where I worked, most of my friends had been black. At the time I was adopted, my stepfather told me a few years later, I'd talked "like an east-shore Negro."

In other words, I knew enough about black people to know, really know, that no black person on the planet could ever like a white person calling her or him that name. And so I also knew what a massive lie Bronco was living.

And it seemed no one else could see this. No one could see what torment the guy was in. I was the youngest, probably the weirdest of Melvin's friends; Melvin and Darlene were like peer parents for a tribe of Lost Boys, guys pushing thirty with no prospects but having lots of fun, getting drunk and stoned, getting laid daily and seemingly at will. I was allowed to hang with the tribe because they were scared of me, scared of how weird I was, and that I'd fight anyone anytime and, they figured, usually win. I kind of looked up to the tribe because they never stopped joking and laughing; they really loved each other.

Everyone certainly loved Bronco; they put him at the center of things and celebrated his idiosyncrasies, especially his relation to that filthy beige cowboy hat. What they didn't see and I could, maybe because I was one myself, was that he was a social freak and knew it, though unlike me he was in torment over that fact. He'd lived his entire life among white people; his entire life, in the eyes of everyone around him, he'd been a representative for a race, its history and cultures, yet was wholly abstracted precisely from that which he represented to everyone around him.

So when Bronco said, "How you be hangin', bro?" without opening his eyes, then reached down and grabbed his hat and placed it over his eyes to shield them from the sunlight I was letting in by entering and not shutting the door, I told him, in a low, friendly voice, that I wasn't his fucking brother and to can the phony talk.

"Yeah, stop talking like a nigger," Warren chimed, sprawled on the carpet and covered head to foot by a yellow sheet; he was spooning with a fifteen-year-old he'd brought to the party. She giggled.

Melvin and Darlene had said the party could continue for another day because it was Sunday and Melvin wouldn't have to go in to run Joey's because the place was getting fumigated; the swabs would have to do without pizzas for one night, and Melvin had chuckled to imagine a clutch of stoned swabs on North Island Naval Air Station discovering that they couldn't get their quota of pies, the horror that would visit their weed-drenched brains.

Everyone more or less roused himself, except for Bronco, who smoked a joint without opening his eyes. "Breakfast of Champions!" he hissed through the smoke.

"Get up, you lazy coon," Warren said, plucking the joint from Bronco.

"Yeah, mazza," Bronco purred, playing yet again Sammy Davis Jr. to Warren's Frank Sinatra. I'd known dudes who'd jack both of them up for acting like that.

Bronco was constantly falling in love with white girls who only wanted to be his friend. He was a good-looking guy, except for his ratty hair and stinky hat, and was very patient in charming women he fancied. He could make them laugh for hours, mostly by pinging off of Warren, doing that ironically racist comedy routine in which Bronco was constantly being referred to as a nigger or coon or jungle bunny.

Irony was supposed to render Bronco the opposite of what he was being referred to as, but the problem was that Bronco and Warren didn't have control of the irony; it whipped around and, to me anyway, had the effect of rendering Bronco precisely what his best friend Warren called him.

Warren's fifteen-year-old had to get home because her parents thought she was staying at a friend's house. Warren pointed out that they were all friends there at Melvin's and Darlene's, and the girl giggled, showed her braces and said Warren knew what she meant, then kissed him quickly and ran outside and jumped on her bicycle. "Old enough to pee, old enough for me," Warren chortled as she peddled off.

Bronco was currently madly in love with Judy Lonzo, a dark, Italian-American beauty Warren said was almost a nigger. I reminded Warren that I was part Greek, and asked if that made me almost one, too. He said that of course it did.

Warren and Bronco spoke pretty good Spanish, and sometimes slipped into it, but slipped out pretty quickly. Neither liked Mexicans much, but went to Baja often to hang out at Warren's parents' beach house. They'd hang for weeks, constantly stoned and eating and drinking on the cheap. They sat at Melvin's and Darlene's kitchen table, passing a joint and talking about going down again next week.

"You gonna ask Judy to come down?" Warren asked Bronco.

"Yeah, man," Bronco said, like it was nothing to ask Judy Lonzo to come down to Baja with him for several days, like there was truly a chance Judy Lonzo would say yes, and join him in Baja and sleep with him every night.

"I think she likes dark meat," Warren said, toking the joint and passing it to me. He was always encouraging his best friend in matters of the heart. They were almost ten years older than I, and I knew they were cool, yet I couldn't help also finding them a little silly. Judy Lonzo was the kind who only dated guys with prospects, those who wanted to be pilots or dentists.

"We had coffee on Friday," Bronco announced in a low, nonchalant voice, and fired up another joint.

"Well, shit, there you go," Warren said.

"She digs jazz," he continued.

"She told you that?" Warren asked.

"Yeah, man. She started ticking off all these jazz groups and I just nodded and smiled like I knew what she was talking about," he said, and Warren cracked up and Bronco smiled big from under the broad brim of his hat, which he was wearing low over his eyes for no good reason except, perhaps, dramatic effect. Bronco's favorite group was Ten Years After.

As they chortled they did one of those fancy handshakes that black guys were no longer doing, or had been doing differently for years. I figured Warren had taught it to Bronco in 1968.

I sat with them for a long time, drinking coffee and smoking joints and cigarettes. Darlene scrambled two cartons of eggs and put a bowl of saltines on the table. We ate and I listened to my older friends talk about people they knew and I didn't, at least in most cases, or not very well. It was thus I learned the lore of Coronado, what Jim Morrison had done and to whom, who played when in what local band that almost made it, who OD'ed and lived to tell about it, and who didn't. Who got busted at the border with twenty ki's. Who actually joined the army and went to Vietnam.

"How'd you guys keep from going?" I asked, realizing it was kind of funny I'd never thought to ask. None of the tribe had gone. What were the odds that a dozen guys of draft age for most of the Sixties right up to 1973, who attended junior colleges sporadically and rarely held jobs, would all get deferments?

"How'd you keep from going?" Bronco shot back.

"Three thirty-nine," I said, quoting my draft lottery number.

"I did what everybody did," Bronco said, picking at his eggs. "School, letters, got a doctor to say I had a pre-existing condition, shit like that. Stall, baby, stall." Bronco and Warren did their antique handshake again. I realized that staying out of the army had been the major achievement of their lives. It was as though everything else was just gravy.

"It's still not too late," Melvin said, scratching his jelly belly with both hands. He'd just gotten out of the shower and had a towel around his hairy middle. He kissed Darlene on the neck and scooped some of her scrambled eggs into his mouth with his fingers.

"Nah, that shit's finished," Warren said resolutely. I knew that Melvin hadn't been drafted because he had a heart murmur. Warren's father was a rich Coronado lawyer who'd been vocally anti-war. He'd joined organizations and gotten his name in the paper a lot. So I didn't bother asking Warren how he kept from going to Vietnam.

I helped Darlene clean up, then had to go to work at the geedunk. That late afternoon I was supposed to teach karate for two hours, but I told them I'd come back with some good weed in the evening.

I peeled off my gee and showered, put on night clothes: a relatively clean shirt and jeans. I walked over to Jimmy's and bought a lid; he dug to the bottom of the box, pulled out a fat one. He was my friend, kind of, and always gave me lots of buds. I paid him with a ten-dollar bill I'd gotten from one of my students, and gave him another five toward the twenty bucks I owed him for two lids he'd fronted me. Jimmy kept half the island in his debt.

It was dusk, and I didn't want to go right over to Melvin's and Darlene's. I wanted to walk around straight for a little while, clear-headed. So I cruised over to the Del and wandered through the lobby, then around to the gift shops and out onto the promenade between the hotel and the tennis courts. I sat on a bench and watched two old men play tennis, two old rich white guys wearing white shorts and shirts and playing pretty well, if getting the ball back over the net to the other guy most of the time constitutes good play. I'd never done tennis, didn't understand the scoring, except that love meant zero. The two old coots were probably in their late fifties, though I wasn't good at guessing the ages of folks past thirty-five or so. They weren't keeping score that I could tell; they were just trying to get the ball back so the other guy could hit it, and they carried on a conversation while they did this, a conversation similarly congenial. They agreed about everything, Nixon, Westmoreland, stagflation, the beauty of the sky as the sun disappeared into the ocean. They seemed like happy men, so I didn't resent their wealth. I only hated a rich person who was bitter, whose bitterness was a pet that accompanied him everywhere, a nasty little manicured poodle some dyspeptic old woman might keep in her abundant lap. The bitter rich assumed they deserved privileges, and, as far as I could tell, hated the un-rich, so hated me.

But those guys knew they had it made. They were thankful and subtle and were rich because they knew how to get along, how to knock the ball back so the other guy could keep hitting it, so the other guy could stay involved.

Nobody had moved, it seemed, and several new people were there, including Judy Lonzo, who was leaning on a guy who looked like a young, very tanned Dick Van Dyke but with long hair tied back tight into a ponytail. He was dressed like someone with prospects. My bet was med school, and sure enough it came out that he was in his third year at UCSD. He was going to be a dermatologist, and was touting sunscreen when most folks thought it was for German tourists and albinos. He took an obligatory hit on a joint to show he wasn't a narc, and then just let them pass.

Judy Lonzo was hot, and very friendly. She had long shiny black hair she was always contending with, swishing this way or that, tucking behind her ears, a terrific and sudden smile and perfect legs. She had a gift for really focusing on you when you talked, nodding and listening intently, and for generally getting people to talk about themselves. She was, therefore, fated for success. And as she leaned back against the future skin doctor's chest, she smiled hugely and listened, really listened to Bronco talking about surf fishing in Baja, and I couldn't believe it when Bronco invited her to come down and stay with him and Warren in the beach house.

She looked puzzled at first, but then said how nice it was of Bronco to invite her and Dick Van Dyke to Warren's parents' beach house; the music was medium loud and Dick Van Dyke was in a conversation with Darlene and obviously didn't get the exchange between Bronco and Judy. Bronco, staring up from the shadow his hat's brim made, forced a smile, toked a roach, and said, yeah, she should talk to the skin doctor later about it, and she said of course she would. He was very busy, and they were thinking of taking a vacation together to Cancun, but maybe a couple of days on the beach in Baja would be nice.

People came and went; Judy and the skin doctor left before nine, which was when Bronco started drinking. Bronco smoked a lot of dope so he wouldn't drink whiskey, which made him crazy, and even Warren got concerned when Bronco broke out the Jack Daniels. Bronco would get entirely wasted once a month, on average, and the way he was hitting the JD this was such an occasion. It was Warren's job to keep him from breaking stuff, keep him from getting killed.

"You don't like Negroes, do you, Rick?" he asked me, but I wasn't taking the bait. He'd done this to me before. When he got drunk and I was around he accused me of not liking Negroes. The fact of the matter was that I just didn't like him.

"You know I'm not like that, Bronco," I mumbled.

"But you really put out a vibe, little bro," he said. I let the brother thing slide.

"You're just picking up static. You should tweak your tuner a little bit when I'm around, Bronco."

"No, no, no, little bro, I know how to read vibes. I'm very sensitive that way." His words poured from the shadow his hat brim cast upon his dark face. He was knocking back the JD, and his voice reminded me of my father's when he was shitfaced, slurred and yet more precise. "I think you've got some fundamental problem with soul brothers."

"Bronco," I sighed, "you're no soul brother."

"And just what the fuck is that supposed to mean?" He was doing his belligerent routine. We'd done this before. Everybody had to go through it at least once with Bronco, but I figured I'd already taken my turn, so resolved not to catch any more flack from him.

"I mean you're one pathetic son of a bitch. You let a rich white boy call you nigger. No soul brother would do that. No dude I've ever known."

The room was struck silent. I'd broken a rule. I'd told Bronco the truth. I could feel everyone's anger; even Melvin and Darlene were mad.

"Get out of here, you low-class little shit," Warren said from behind me. I turned to look at him. He was gritting his teeth. He loved Bronco. "Tell him to get the fuck out," Warren said to Melvin. But to Melvin's credit he just tried to tamp everything down. He mumbled something about everybody getting along, that life was too short to waste any of it on anger.

"You ever even talked to another black guy besides Bronco?" I asked Warren.

He told me to kiss his ass. He was getting bold. Bronco guzzled the JD directly from the bottle. He was speechless.

"Have you ever talked to a soul brother?" I asked Bronco. "You ever hang out with a real soul brother?" I didn't want to leave under such circumstances, but everybody wanted me gone, so I rose from the kitchen chair, walked past Warren, brushing him hard. It was he I found disgusting, though I wasn't even entirely sure why. He was a nice guy, a loyal friend. He and I had always gotten along. Bronco and I had always gotten along. I was losing an entire set of friends. I had a sudden urge to turn and apologize, even beg forgiveness. But I couldn't. Something wasn't right. I didn't know how to say it; I didn't understand what was wrong, but I knew that love shouldn't cost that much.

STATIC
SUMMER, 1974

Tim passed me a joint. I clipped it with one of his red-feather crocodiles, hit it, two, three, four times, passed it back. "Twenty kilos?" I said, exhaling hugely.

"Yeah," he said, and I waited for more, but there was never more from Tim. He was a guy of almost no words. Everything he did say was meant to resonate far beyond the usual parameters of stoned chatter. You just had to get used to that.

"Spacey Fred has the contacts all lined up, and he's fronting for the ki's, most of them, anyway, right?" This I'd gleaned from Spacey Fred before coming over to Tim's to give him his karate lesson, and to discuss further the business proposal Fred had presented.

"Yep," he chirped, holding the smoke.

"I get a thousand bucks no matter what?"

He nodded.

"All I have to do is ride shotgun, do a little driving?"

He smiled.

"Grand Forks, North Dakota? Isn't that a suburb of the North Pole?"

He laughed, choking out a little smoke.

"I don't have to touch the shit, right? I mean, if we get caught, I can say I didn't even know it was in the car, right? You guys pack it, I never even see it, deal? I'm just going to Grand Forks, North Dakota, for a vacation."

This cracked Tim up. He thought I was joking.

Louanna was nuts and driving me likewise. I had next to nothing in my savings account. I needed some adventure, a nice road trip, and a thousand bucks would get me well.

Tim was a Buddhist who'd never actually met another Buddhist, but had taught himself the religion from two books, one that consisted largely of photographs. He'd begun to teach himself karate similarly, but had hooked up with me, so was receiving quite good instruction. He lived on a stipend he got from a trust fund one of his grandmothers had set up for him. He would receive $310 a month more or less for the rest of his life. I envied him deeply. He owned an old beige Volvo that would serve as our means of transport across the deserts and plains of America. He'd invested some of his own money into the kilos, but Spacey Fred, who'd never fully recovered from overdosing on Dramamine, of all things, had invested the most.

Tim lit some incense before his shrine to Buddha, an emerald-green fat and laughing fellow made of porcelain. After I'd leave, he'd do his meditation. I'd tried to explain to him that you can't really meditate stoned, and he'd just smiled.

Tim possessed sculpted muscles, long stringy brown hair and coke-bottle glasses. He sat full-lotus with his shirt off. I said, "You realize you're staking your life on the organizational skills of a thirty-year-old janitor? A guy who managed to OD on Dramamine? A guy who once snorted a quarter ounce of powdered sugar, then went back and bought some more?" Spacey Fred was famous for getting ripped off. He'd smoked more oregano than anyone on earth.

"We got the shit," Tim said. I mulled this over. He was saying that he'd already purchased the kilos of powerful Panama Red, that Fred had already put up his larger portion of the cash. The car was gassed, the contacts on the other side hot and ready. All we had to do was hit the road. He was also saying that I worried too much, that I just had to enter the slipstream of my fate, ride the currents. Maybe all he meant was, "We got the shit," but I needed more, and with Tim one could construe.

I especially needed to get out of Coronado, not just for the week and a half or so the trip would take, but forever. When guys got just a little older than I without making the break, they never got out. They became like Spacey Fred, or the Tribe, the gang of guys in their late twenties and early thirties who were all good-looking and cool and got laid a lot, but who were moochers and drunks and would never fit in anywhere else. I didn't want to join the Tribe, work in restaurants, live in garage apartments, or with other guys, into my late twenties. Most of them were waiting around for their parents to die so they could inherit enough to move down to Mexico forever. They were always talking about moving down to Mexico forever, living the good life there among people they otherwise loathed, the Mexicans. They never talked about waiting for their parents to die, but each could tell you the official appraised value of his ancestral home, and of the automobiles each of his parents drove.

And I certainly didn't want to wake up on my thirtieth birthday as a janitor of a Catholic grammar school or of a geedunk on the Amphibious Base, where I was then indeed a janitor. That afternoon I informed my boss Esther Hale that I'd be gone for ten days, and that I'd arrange for one of the guys in the PX to pick up my shifts. She asked me why I was taking off and I told her I needed a vacation.

We met at Tim's at 4 a.m.; I hadn't slept, even after Louanna had drifted off at around two, because once I'd lain still a few minutes all I could think was that I'd spend the next several days sitting on, literally, twenty kilos of powerful weed, enough that if we got caught we'd certainly go to prison for a long time. So, this is how it begins, I'd thought. This is how the beginning of a huge, life-changing fuck-up feels. And yet I'd committed, and if I backed out and the whole thing went off without a hitch I'd feel like an incredible chickenshit. I'd hate myself. Tim would certainly hate me for being a coward. Spacey Fred wouldn't know the difference, but that didn't matter.

So I committed to the trip as an opportunity to prove to myself that I wasn't a coward, and showed up at four, sleepy but wired on NoDoz and dread. I'd had ridiculous goodbye sex with Louanna all night, and if nothing else the trip would be a rest from that. Fred was eating a cheeseburger. He'd bought nine for the trip, kept them stacked in their paper wrappers in a cooler with a box of saltines, three apples, a six-pack of Blue Ribbon, a quart of liquid protein, and no ice.

Tim had a change of shorts and two tee-shirts, a battery of vitamins, and a bottle of Jack Daniel's. I brought a fey little suitcase I'd spied in a dumpster, a pink cardboard number. Tim and Fred laughed at it. I had three changes of clothes in it, clean underwear even, and wondered if I'd be allowed to take my clean underwear to prison. I'd gotten the eighty-seven dollars I had to my name out of the bank and from a little hole behind the fridge. Louanna had given me thirty dollars more, and her qualified blessing to take the trip, not that I needed it at that point. I hoped she wouldn't kill herself while I was gone, but not enough to stay and monitor the situation. I needed not to be a coward, and would therefore take that trip no matter what. I especially needed to get away from her, but didn't have the courage simply to walk out for no other reason than to be away from her.

Fred insisted upon driving first, and we kept having to remind him of the basics, like press down on the gas to go. He had no problem shifting gears, but seemed not to know when to stop for a red light. He'd brake whenever he saw the red light, even if it were three blocks away. Tim thought it was hilarious; I tried to laugh, but at 4:20 a.m. on dark Orange Avenue I didn't find anything hilarious, much less the prospect of prison, where guys fucked guys and where I'd be much too pretty to get away with acting tough, and where the first time I tried I'd get bum rushed and gang raped. "Black belt in karate?" I could imagine some burly lifer chuckling. "Well, sweetie pie, I got a blue ribbon once for catching a greased pig…"

"Let's talk about prison," I said.

"Why?" Fred asked.

"Because I want to know that both of you understand federal prison's where we're headed if we get stopped and twenty kilos of Panama Red, which I know absolutely nothing about, suddenly appear."

"Bummer," Fred said.

"No, it's a bummer when you find half a cockroach in your enchilada. Getting busted with twenty kilos is a tad closer to a disaster of biblical proportions." They loved it when I talked like that. Tim wouldn't stop chortling. Fred had no idea what I was saying, but he was smiling, cruising over the blue arching Coronado Bridge, a song in his heart it seemed from how he bopped his head and rocked it back and forth as though to some sassy tune. I'd made it clear that I was in charge of music, and would not allow any in the car until we were out of the city. I wanted to keep all distractions to a minimum, though I had no control over what was going on in Spacey Fred's head, and whatever it was kept his otherwise vacant face bopping and swiveling, and every few seconds he drummed a little riff on the steering wheel.

I'd run a kilo or two to the Bay Area, so I was no virgin to such crime. But this was clearly a different kind of situation. On my runs to Berkeley I'd been little more than chump. This was the sort of thing you read about in newspapers. We were a blue marlin, the kind of drug run a narc could stuff and proudly mount on his wall.

And how did Tim and Fred get the ki's? How did they know they hadn't been set up? "Who'd you buy these kilos I don't know about from?" I asked Tim.

"Ask Fred," he said.

"Who'd you get these kilos from?" I asked Fred.

"Juan Gomez," he said, filling me with terror. Juan Gomez, a former SEAL team member who preferred to deal in everything but marijuana, was as notorious a narc as he was a dealer. Getting Spacey Fred busted was precisely the sort of thing he'd do to satisfy his narc handlers so he could continue to do his real business.

"I can't believe you got over forty pounds of marijuana from the biggest fucking narc this side of Fresno." I was trying to control my voice, my anger, my terror.

"He likes me," Fred said.

"What do you mean, Juan Gomez likes you? He's an animal, a predator. How'd you know he had the shit?"

"Mindy told me," he replied. Mindy was Juan Gomez's very pretty, classy girlfriend no one could believe was still with him given how many times he'd slapped her silly in public.

"When did you ever talk to Mindy Lewis?" Juan Gomez had beaten guys half to death, including a couple of his close friends, for looking at her for four seconds. No one was allowed to look at her for more than three.

"Mindy and me are old friends," Fred announced, smiling. Harbinger of doom, dawn glorified the distant mountains.

"How's that?"

"We grew up next door to each other on A Avenue. We used to play all the time. She had a swing set in her backyard. Her daddy and my daddy was best friends. And before my mom died she was best friends with Mindy's mom."

There was a lot to unpack there, and I didn't even want to start. But I did still need to know why Mindy Lewis hooked Fred up with Juan Gomez for a substantial drug deal. "Fred, start from the beginning. How'd you know Mindy could help you score kilos from Juan Gomez?"

"She kind of told me at school," Fred said. Mindy taught fourth grade at the Sacred Heart School where Fred was janitor.

"Fred, you're telling me Mindy Lewis discussed your getting twenty kilos of Panama Red from Juan Gomez while her fourth graders played dodge ball at recess?"

"No, we was in the lunch hall. We're old friends. We can talk about anything anywhere. She just told me she needed me to help her out." We were getting into some morning traffic, but would miss the nasty stuff if we didn't dawdle.

"You are to remain in the middle lane, no matter what, Fred. No passing, no lane changing. You dig?"

"Yeah," he said. Fred was scared of me.

"So, like, what did she need help with?" I asked.

"She needed some money."

I waited as long as I could. "Come on, Fred, fucking elaborate."

"Huh?"

"You helped her get money?"

"Sure," he smiled. "I bought the dope."

"You bought twenty kilos from Mindy Lewis?"

"Yeah, we're old friends. She needed money and I needed the dope."

"I thought you said this was Juan Gomez's dope."

"It was."

"But Mindy sold it to you."

"Yeah."

By the time we were in the desert, I'd somehow pried enough out of Spacey Fred to have a pretty good idea of what had happened. Mindy Lewis had ripped off Juan Gomez. She'd let the guy publicly humiliate her for years, and had been ripping him off steadily. She hadn't needed the money; she'd just wanted it. The way she was doing it, if anything ever went wrong, Juan Gomez would most likely take the fall. According to Fred, or at least according to what I could surmise from my two-hour interrogation, Juan Gomez had taken the twenty kilos from a Mexican who owed him in a cocaine deal that had gone funny. That is, he'd beaten the guy unconscious and taken his dope. He'd put the ki's in the trunk of Mindy's Ferrari, and Mindy had simply told Spacey Fred to pry open her trunk with a crowbar and take the dope, then to put the money in an envelope and drop it in her mailbox. Of course, Juan Gomez would think the Mexican he'd beaten unconscious had simply stolen back his dope, and would continue to think so even as the guy pleaded for his life and vigorously denied having broken into the Ferrari.

Word was always out that someone had ripped off Juan Gomez and had better be halfway to Sydney, Australia, because Juan Gomez was looking for him. Juan Gomez was always ripping off dealers he said had ripped him off. Juan Gomez was always getting drunk at the Mexican Village with his buddies and their wives and girlfriends after the guys had played rugby in Star Park; on those occasions, he would always punch one of his buddies for staring at Mindy Lewis for too long, and then slap the hell out of her for getting stared at. She was tall; she had dark brown hair down to her shoulders and powder-blue eyes. Everything about her was precise; her bangs were precisely cut a half-inch above her precisely plucked eyebrows. Her make-up was applied precisely, was never smeared or faded. She dressed like a schoolteacher, even when she was in the Mexican Village swilling pitchers of Margaritas with Juan Gomez and his posse of sycophants. She was severely pretty, not beautiful. There was something oddly mannish in her angular prettiness, the precision of it.

As we rolled through the desert in the late morning I knew that nothing good would come of the trip, but neither would anything particularly bad come of it. I knew I'd be lucky enough to climb out of it without getting arrested. I knew that Fred's "contacts" were all in his head. I knew that in a few years Tim would manage a Pier One in Fashion Valley or Mission Valley or the Valley of Lost Souls just north of Sand Through Your Fingers. Fred would run for mayor of Fred against a ghost of his former self and lose by a narrow margin. Juan Gomez would buy the franchises to several Midas Mufflers in Chula Vista and National City and one day see the face of Jesus in a pool of forty-weight. Mindy Lewis would marry a lieutenant commander and produce several heartless daughters. Juan Gomez's powerful dope would be disseminated through the youth population of Grand Forks, North Dakota, and I knew that my own charmed life was the dance of sunlight on dull chrome, the long flash of recognition in a desert of probabilities, one in which my best play may have been simply to flip on the radio and listen to the static, the stars, except that the guy beside me had had a tune in his head for hours, doing a little dance behind the wheel, drumming, swaying, bopping, and I wished I could hear it, too.

THE ACID GAME
SPRING, 1974

An all-night poker game on acid sounded like a good idea, though even straight I played just well enough to lose lots of money, to Barney, mostly, but to the other guys as well. Oh, I sometimes won, sometimes walked away with a few bucks and my head held high, but usually didn't. Barney was born to gamble; he was smart that way.

To get into the acid game you had to have a hundred dollars, a significant amount, but since there was a fifty-cent limit you'd almost have to want to lose everything actually to do so. A tab of acid, and all the beer you could drink and Fritos and onion dip you could eat were free. Barney was a classy guy.

So the six of us took the Windowpane, toasted with sixteen-ouncers, and sat down to Barney's kitchen table, which had been my kitchen table after I'd stolen it from Chris who'd bought it at a garage sale in Chula Vista and owed me money. It had angel decals in each corner, naked winged babies blowing long skinny horns of gold.

Phil started off with one of his goddamned goofy high-low games in which more cards were wild than weren't; such games always took eons and two guys usually split a measly pot because no one liked to venture much in a high-low situation. If you stuck it out you could lose a lot, but usually not make much.

Then Peter wanted to play Indian poker and everyone groaned and begged him not to, but we ended up holding the cards up to our foreheads and of course everyone cheated.

Finally, the deal got to Barney, who was ready to infuse a little sanity, and dignity, into the game: Seven-card stud, nothing wild, no bullshit. It got interesting quickly.

Barney had a bullet showing; I had two kings, and everybody else garbage, though Phil raised with a four of hearts showing, which meant he had another four buried, a couple of same-face cards down, no better than queens I hoped, or was starting to come on to the acid, like I was, and just raised because he felt utterly alone in the universe. The way he stared at his up card, mouth slightly agape, pupils huge and wild, I went with the latter and resolved to discount everything he did after that.

Peter folded because in about fourteen years he would be a proctologist married to a devout Seventh-Day Adventist, and their four ugly children would all be covered with freckles.

"Why'd you fold, Pete?" Barney asked. "Jesus, you've only seen three cards."

"I don't know," he mumbled, "the way Phil raised..."

Barney got a ten of spades to go with his ace of spades; I got another king. Everybody else got trash. Phil raised, staring right at my two kings showing. I should have known better than to say anything, but blurted,

"Phil, what are you doing?" Barney shushed me. If Phil was sucking Ishtar's cosmic tit and wanted to cast off his earthy wealth, Barney was glad to scoop it up. Barney had no problem taking his friends' money. I did, but I was a chump and everybody knew it.

Robby got my fourth king, Barney a queen of spades, Phil got another four, Dave got trash and folded, and I got my full house with another eight.

I was sparking, seeing trails. Barney's hair was mussed and he looked like he had horns. Yes, Barney was a devil of sorts; I'd always known that, found it the most endearing aspect of his nature, how he was always on the make, always on the lookout for a smooth scam, a quick buck, the next juicy sucker. And yet he had a good heart.

Both of our birth mothers were dead. His father married, after Barney moved out, a great woman whom Barney didn't like but all his friends loved, and my stepmother was an angry gay truckdriver trapped in a housewife's sagging body. Barney and I had lived together briefly; I'd moved out after an argument that ensued when I ate the frozen shrimp he'd bought to use as bait down at the pier on the bay. Unemployed, he'd resolved to live solely on what he could catch, cadge, and win at poker. He'd pulled it off for several months.

Robby tapped his fingers. Phil wouldn't blink. I stared at him for twenty seconds or two minutes and he didn't blink. Finally, I said, "Fucking blink, Phil," and he looked at me then stared off again, unblinking. No one else registered that I'd said anything. "Robby, would you stop that," I added, "you're driving me nuts."

"We're all nuts," Phil said, only his mouth moving. Robby tapped faster. Then Phil raised. I raised him. Barney raised me.

Barney got a nine of spades. Phil got another four. It didn't matter what I got, and what Robby was doing just didn't make sense. Everybody raised right up to the limit. The pot was enormous.

After the hole cards I studied my friends', my adversaries', faces. Barney's horns had lengthened, turned red and curved forward. They looked lethal. His face said only that in twenty years he'd be doing almost exactly what he was now doing, only more desperately, efficiently. Phil was cruising the craters of the moon, skimming the vacuum as sleek as a seal, a song in his heart, something off of *Weasels Ripped My Flesh*, or just about anything else by Frank Zappa. Robby stared at his cards as he would one day stare into actuary tables, with the dispassionate reverence of a man born to sell insurance. Dave would be dead in a few years, something medical, but now he was just tripping, happy, and lucky, to have folded. Peter was peering into the hole of his empty Coors can, his brow wrinkled.

This was why I was so bad at poker, why I played just well enough to lose to Barney almost always. I had a king-high full house, and I was getting spooked. With such a hand, one simply had to throw oneself into the winds of fate. Yeah, Barney probably had his flush, and Phil may even have fallen into a vat of angel shit and arisen from it smelling like four of a kind. Robby was probably holding the mangy tail of a black hole, the flea-infested fur of contingency. But I had to stick with that king-high full house, the sort of hand one is dealt in Hell again and again and again and again and again, show it the kind of loyalty only the higher orders of angels are programmed to sing.

"I'd like a portable pussy," Phil mumbled.

"Say what?" someone said.

"A pussy, a real one, you could just kind of take places," Phil added.

"That's disgusting," Robby said, and I nodded agreement.

"You're sick," Barney said, and the rest of us nodded.

"Why is that so farfetched?" Phil asked. He was hitting his philosophical phase early.

"Because it just isn't right," I said. I was reading *The Feminine Mystique* for a Women in Literature class at State. I'd signed up for it primarily to meet more women, but Sally Collins had become my favorite professor. "You can't make a fetish of parts of women's bodies, Phil. That's one of the reasons the world's so fucked up."

"The world's fucked up because I want a portable pussy?" Phil asked, his face oddly serene.

"It's a symptom, Phil. A symptom," I answered.

"You don't think there are girls who'd like portable penises?" Phil pressed.

"Well, some do have dildos," Robby added in the spirit of fairness.

"It's not the same thing!" I yelled.

"Why not?" Barney asked. The tide was turning in Phil's favor.

I was stumped. What indeed was the difference between a dildo and a portable vagina? I almost launched into a history lesson, something about the historical oppression of women, about how breasts were used to sell everything, and about the important fact that women didn't rape and generally brutalize men. I almost said that one way guys got their heads prepared for rape was to objectify the woman's body, precisely as Phil now did, fantasizing about his portable vagina. If I'd said all that, and Professor Collins had been standing there listening, she'd have been proud of me, and maybe she'd have had sex with me. She was hot, mid-thirties, smart, funny, really pretty. But I just said, "We're all pigs," and as I glanced around the room my friends' resemblance to actual pigs became striking, especially Phil's with his tiny eyes and pushed-in nose. Robby crammed his snout with Fritos and Barnie was a porker with horns. On the far wall, in separate posters, Jeff Beck and Alvin Lee stood side by side playing guitars, looking for all the world like cool swine.

"Oink," Peter said, and the others sniggered. My friends thought I was a pretentious ass for saying all that Women's Lib stuff, but I hadn't said it, only thought it. Or had I actually said it and thought I was only thinking? Why had Peter, who'd checked out of the conversation as soon as he'd folded, suddenly said something clever? But on second thought it wasn't that clever.

"Oink? That's the best you can do?" I said.

"Lighten up, Reverend," Barney said. When anybody got serious Barnie called him Reverend. The only thing anyone was supposed to be serious about was the game, any game Barney was in, anyway.

"Just don't poke me with those things," I said, attempting to lighten up, but then realized that maybe not everyone saw Barney's horns, though they looked long and sharp enough to open a can of tuna. "You got any tunafish around here?" I asked Barney.

"Why don't you just go in there and eat my fucking bait," Barney said, pointing his chin at the kitchen, and everyone cracked up. Their piggy faces were purple.

"I didn't know it was your bait, Barney," I said, much too seriously. Barney was long past being angry about it. Besides, my eating his bait had simply been the tip of the domestic iceberg. The main problems had been two: he was a bigger slob than I, and I was constantly harping on him about that, and we'd made a deal in the beginning that whoever brought a girl back to the apartment got the bedroom even though it was Barney's bed. But then I'd hit a winning streak and was bringing girls back to the apartment two or three nights a week. So when I boiled his bait, and he came home and saw me eating it with saltines and Tabasco, he stole my car and didn't give it back for days.

"Hey, let's raise the limit," Phil said.

"To what?" Barney asked.

"To nothing," Phil said, but nobody got what he was saying, except Barney, who grew a malevolent smile. His face was magenta. His horns seemed to glitter a little.

Then I got it. Phil wanted to take the limit off the bets completely. "For the rest of the night?" I said, stupidly.

"There won't be a rest of the night," Barney purred, because of course if we were going where Phil was trying to take us, there wouldn't be another hand. "And no owsies, right? We bet what we brought?" I asked for clarification. I craved tuna. I stuck a five-dollar bill in my shirt pocket. When this was finished, I would have a nice tunafish sandwich at the Nite & Day, with fries and a big pickle. I reached into the cooler and pulled out another Coors. I was suddenly parched, so drained it, popped another.

I was sure we'd finished the betting about thirty-two years ago, and we probably had, but we were going another round, anyway. I was stuck, but wouldn't raise, would just call everybody else's raises.

And so it went right to the predictable conclusion, when everyone but the future ass doctor had everything in the pot, but Phil wasn't finished. He did something extraordinary. He fished his key ring out of his pocket, peeled the key of his '57 Chevy off of it, and threw it into the pot.

His brother Dean had given it to him before shipping out to Vietnam. It was cherry. Phil had taken good care of it, as a kind of tribute.

"You can't do that," I said.

"Why not?" Barney asked, smiling, so cool. "We said anything we brought to the table," and raised his butt to pull from his jeans the key to the '65 Chrysler he'd just bought from a rich hippie in La Jolla. I'd had in mind, of course, what that '57 Chevy represented rather than cars in general, but didn't want to make that argument. It was too complicated. Robby folded without a whimper. He was staring into the red glow of his cigarette, blowing on it lightly to make it brighten.

Barney had his flush, and Phil either had four fours, some kind of low full house, or was simply preparing to take a one-way walk into high tide.

I pulled the key to my Mercury station wagon—that I'd just gotten fixed, the carburetor rebuilt and the brakes made somewhat legal—from my pants, then said, "I'm out," and clutched my key.

Of course Barney had his flush, but Phil had some chump-change four-high full house. There was much cursing and laughing and arm-punching, until Phil reached into his pocket and pulled out another key. "Good thing I brought my spare," he smiled, and at first nobody got it except Barney, but then it dawned on the rest of us.

"You can't do that!" Robby screamed.

"I want my money back. You owe me, douche bag," I yelled. Phil had a zit in the corner of his mouth. He seemed always to have a zit in the corner of his mouth, and he was laughing so hard he couldn't breathe. Barney just smiled and shook his head at Phil betting his key, not his car.

"You got me there, pal," he said to Phil, and popped him on the back to help him get his breath. "I'll even let you have your key back," he added, and tossed it gently in front of Phil on the table. Barney appreciated a good scam. Phil had probably been planning this since puberty, about the same time Barney started winning most of Phil's money at cards. If he'd won, Phil would have kept the cars. But technically all he'd bet was his key, and we'd all agreed that the only thing at stake was what we had brought to the table.

GRUNION
SPRING, 1973

Nixon was coming. Orange Avenue was packed ten-deep on both sidewalks in anticipation of the motorcade. I stood on the steps of the Coronado Public Library, a good spot to see the President of the United States, whom I hated from my gut.

My politics were inchoate; I was nineteen and plugged into mushy counterculture sentiments, and had begun to puzzle through lefty theory that sounded swell to the degree I understood any of it, which was a gnat's ass more than not at all. But my loathing of Richard Millhouse Nixon was something in my blood, not my head.

And I wasn't a hater; I wasn't someone with an extensive shit list. I didn't hold grudges, and soon forgot slights. I was disdainful of all the right things: the KKK, a.m. radio, salesmen, Nazis, television, Republicans, Christmas, anything which seemed to jive with Lawrence Welk's bubble machine, the idea of it. But that was all in my head. What I felt for Nixon surfed the currents in my veins.

I had no idea why I felt such deep loathing for him. He'd never done anything to me personally; he'd scored points on the Great Wall and did not seem in a hurry to start World War Three. Even Vietnam was winding down, so I wouldn't have to go. I resented that he'd gotten reelected in a landslide, but that was just American democracy in action: you choose between two guys who've been tapped by two small groups that run everything, so whoever wins has the hand of Special Interest up his ass bouncing him through the Punch and Judy of governance. I knew it wouldn't have been much different with McGovern, though I'd voted for him with great excitement just a few months earlier, actually thinking he'd had a chance.

It probably had to do with the fact that Nixon was a Dick, like my father; it may have been that simple. The loathing I felt for my father, my desire to beat Daddy Dick to death with my fists, I'd somehow transferred by the alchemy of the unconscious onto poor Tricky Dick. I'd just begun my extensive misreading of Freud, and so had some inkling even at the time that in my psyche the two Dicks were linked.

The motorcade turned from Third Avenue and oozed south. He stood up in the car and waved and smiled more winningly than he ever had on television. He chanced such a juicy head shot because he was among the faithful, on Coronado Island, cushioned between two huge military bases of which he was commander-in-chief, in the midst of a population that thought he was a little too left-wing, but better than the alternative, so cheered their ultra-conservative asses off. I got chills when Dick Nixon looked right at me and dipped his chin and waved.

In 1989 I'd have a half-hour conversation with George W. Bush on St. Charles Avenue in New Orleans, during the Bacchus parade on that Saturday before Fat Tuesday; he was just the president's goofy son who was minority owner of a baseball team. He'd come over from Texas to help out the guy running against David Duke for the Republican nomination for a state senate seat. George and I had grabbed the same string of beads from the air and I'd ripped his end from his hand. He was very gracious about it when I turned to look at whom I'd defeated and recognized him; he was chatty, innocuous, a nice guy. Of course I had no idea he'd be president in about a decade. The event registered at the same frequency as when I met the first lead singer of Iron Butterfly, a crystalline tenor who'd quit just before the group acquired a gritty baritone and recorded its one and only monster hit.

But when Dick Nixon looked into my eyes and dipped his chin and waved I gasped and tingled, for my existence had never been, and I realized would never be again, acknowledged by a being of such historic proportions. Dick Nixon's name would live forever, for he was a man of such power that decisions he made would resonate to the end of time, even if he was a sweaty reptile, even though he had the hand of Special Interest up his ass dancing him through a more or less rightwing agenda. So my loathing got mixed with awe, and therefore got more complicated, too, and perhaps even closer in type to what I felt for my father.

I hated my father for the wrong reasons back then; it would take me years to learn to hate him for the right reasons, and then finally to exit altogether that condition of spirit, and that was my exit from youth. My father was a sick man, which is to say he was passionate but unable to love. Loveless passion is a rudderless existence, and he drove randomly all over America, bouncing checks, committing innumerable small crimes, making children with a beautiful soul-sick woman until he was caught and sent to prison, then caught again and again sent to prison. I hated my father for being a failure, and yet he hadn't been. He'd been successful at the only thing his diseased nature would allow him to do: to move randomly and daily, and cover his tracks. He'd brutalized me from time to time, but hadn't wanted to. He was unable to love, but in the drift of his objectless passion did not require the solace of physical dominance. He could be brutal when impatient, and his patience with children could evaporate in seconds.

When Watergate hit the fan, I was living with Louanna, a gorgeous, mildly suicidal woman who was head over heels for the French language, and otherwise still loved her sexually dysfunctional ex-husband and used me as a kind of sex toy. I was nineteen, so happy to be thus exploited. We both attended San Diego City College, commuting from Coronado. I took mostly literature courses, among them a Greek mythology course in which Cameron Crowe was my classroom buddy; he was slightly younger than I but already a kind of hotshot rock and roll reporter, though unnaturally humble about it; I also took a history course each of my two semesters, one from Harry and the other from Larry.

The courses were the first and second semesters of American History, but that's not what Harry and Larry taught; they taught Watergate I and II. They watched the hearings each day and explained them to us in minute detail, and then, with broad strokes, placed events into a New Left historical perspective. At the end of the semester Harry asked each of us what grade he or she wanted. Larry actually gave us a lame test and assigned everyone an A who remembered to put her or his name on the test sheet, which was nearly half the class.

Harry and Larry were terrific friends to one another, very bright guys in their early forties (Harry turned forty that fall semester) with M.A. degrees probably from decent universities. My guess now is that they'd both been brilliant Ph.D. students who'd simply said screw it and then got stuck on the junior college circuit. They woke up together at the dawn of midlife, their academic careers in the toilet, and decided simply to have fun, mainly at Dick Nixon's expense. Harry was a rakishly handsome blue-eyed blond WASP, Larry a goofy New York Jew with coke-bottle glasses and long greasy-black hair. Both had incredibly infectious smiles, and spent almost every hour they weren't in class drinking pitchers of beer with students at the fabled watering hole across the street from the campus, where the TV above the bar was tuned in hourly to the Watergate hearings.

I liked both those men very much, just as everyone else did. They broke down barriers between the classroom and the world, between categories of knowledge, and between institutional roles. They turned their "courses" into one great symposium centered on the historical moment, yet referring back always to sources and their greater contexts. It was personality-centered pedagogy, but because they were sincere, knowledgeable, and truly humble toward their students, it worked at that moment, under those circumstances. There were Harrys and Larrys throughout higher education then, and some of them were authentic and some bogus. I'm not sure that kind of act can work anymore, but it did then, and to great effect.

Harry and Larry were stars, especially in the bar; everyone wanted to be close to them when the beer was flowing and they were on a roll, goofing on Nixon, goofing on America and each other. I was pretty far down the student pecking order; there were lots of guys going to City College on the GI Bill, older guys and older women who worked real jobs, had kids, and could talk to Harry and Larry more or less as peers, and I didn't try to elbow my way to the front of that queue, but sometimes it would work out that I'd be sitting close to Harry or Larry and would actually get a few words into the raucous, jovial conversation they were leading, and which at its core was as substantive as any good seminar discussion.

"He looked at me," I blurted.

"What do you mean?" Larry asked. The noise in the bar was considerable. Everyone was talking back to the TV, and it was turned up loud. The Watergate hearings, for that crowd, were like a sports event.

Larry was being polite. There were two other conversations going on, one being led by Harry that he wanted to wedge into. I knew it, and realized I probably shouldn't have said anything.

"Nothing, Larry," I mumbled, and sipped my beer, which I was too young to be drinking in a bar. But I'd captured his interest.

"Nixon? Nixon looked at you?"

Harry and two vets heard this and stopped yelling at each other and the TV. I'd spoken from some semi-dream state; the beer had made me say it, the beer and my desire to engage those beautiful men, to have them hear me.

"It was no big deal," I said, dropping my chin.

"He was talking about Nixon?" Harry said to Larry.

"It was weird," I said. "He looked right at me and waved. We made eye contact. I ate some mushrooms about an hour earlier. Pretty mild shit. And I was just standing there on the steps, the library steps in Coronado. Remember when he went there? And, like, I really hate the son-of-a-bitch but when he looked at me and smiled…" I had no idea where I was going with that. I knew I'd screwed up saying anything about it at all. I had no thesis, no point. I was shedding no light on Sam Nunn's motives, or upon the issue of the efficacy of the Independent Council. I was nineteen and talking about my pain, about my love for my father, about how much I'd missed him when I was a child and he was in prison. Of course I didn't know that's what I was talking about, but somehow Harry and Larry did, because they were genuine teachers, and knew that the subtext of history is written in the sand of our hearts.

When the grunion ran in spring, my buddies and I would get stoned and chase them with flashlights. We'd dig holes in the sand, great bowls, and drop them by the handful into it. In the moonlight, the thousands, millions of little bodies were writhing silver. Folks said they were edible. Barney once froze some, then battered and floured them and dropped them into Crisco. He set a platter of them before us, his stoned friends, and Phil actually ate one.

But grunion are only edible in the sense that anything not poisonous is edible. They're not for eating, but for chasing. The morning after a grunion run the beach is an ancient text of their passage from one world into another and back. And we who vexed them as they were reproducing, galloping between worlds, between conditions, were only minor agents of fate.

THE SERAPHS
SPRING, 1974

They gathered unto themselves, spoke their own language. The tides were in their blood, and their desires simple and strong. Small gestures among them often supplanted words; and they were all beautiful, in a certain way.

Which is to say most were blond and blue-eyed. I didn't think much about ethnicity then, but sometimes they mistook me for a Mexican, and treated me with the mild disdain they expressed toward Mexicans and Chicanos, anyone swarthy for reasons other than constant exposure to the sun, so I felt wholly other than the surfers, who occupied the highest station in the youth social order of Coronado, California.

And yet, to their great credit, they existed among us with an easy grace that seemed by turns patrician equanimity and bored dismissal. I thought most of them were idiots, but admired them, for they were profoundly untroubled. All of life's importance was reduced to one thing; all else was tangential to it, and that one thing had no great point. A body could not win, except that managing not to fall was success, and so a body could not lose, except that every moment not standing upon the rolling tides was a lesser existence.

I was too young to be a father. I was twenty, but fifteen years too young to center my life upon raising a child. When Corry got around to telling me she was pregnant, she was well into her second trimester. I'd beg her to tell her mother, but she'd go blank when I did, utterly blank. I threatened to tell her mother, but she remained blank. I threatened to tell her father and she simply turned away. She told me she wanted to have the baby. I could hang around or not.

Corry was gorgeous, a little Latin-seeming, small, dark, voluptuous. She turned eighteen just a few weeks before I learned she was pregnant. She was very smart, but hated school. She hated everything but applying makeup and talking about having kids. I'd gotten tangled up with her because she was gorgeous, and because her mother fed me and let me crash downstairs on the couch many nights, which was convenient since I had no place of my own in which to sleep. Her mother owned several thriving beauty parlors in San Diego, Escondido, and Palm Springs. Her stepfather was a civilian subcontractor on North Island Naval Air Station, and a drunk. It took me a while to realize how much emotional effort that man expended tolerating my presence in his life over those months, how decent, despairingly patient, he was.

I had two other places to crash. Sometimes I slept on a pallet of army-surplus blankets in the kitchen of the Coronado Tea Garden; I'd clean up around the place in the evenings so they gave me a key to one of the two padlocks on the backdoor; if they didn't want me to stay there for whatever reason on a particular night, they simply used the other lock, so

I always had to have a backup, and it was usually Mr. Clean's tool shed.

Mr. Clean was what we called the swab who was one of my regular karate students; he was in his late thirties, was close to a twenty-year retirement which he constantly talked about, though the guy was a real lifer, would certainly go for thirty. He was an E5, a second-class petty officer who had a more or less permanent billet on North Island. As is said of some convicts, he stayed in because he couldn't have functioned on the outside, though he yammered about getting out, being free of the Navy, all its candy-ass rules. He rented a run-down house at the wrong end of Orange Avenue, the north end, closest to the bay and the base. He shaved his head and hence the nickname. He was the most emotionally stunted man his age I'd ever encountered. But he let me use his backyard to give lessons, and he let me crash in his toolshed, into which I'd dragged a mattress about the time I'd lost my apartment and met Corry in fast succession.

I actually had a little money, but didn't want to get settled into another place on the island. I wanted to move out by San Diego State where I was more or less making progress towards a degree, and wanted to save up for that move. I knew that if I got settled in again, got another garage apartment or moved in with some guys, I'd prolong my departure from Coronado, and I desired mightily to get off the island, to get away from the geedunk where I was janitor; away from my karate students for whom I felt responsible and with whom I was bored; away from my stepmother who could conjure from my depths massive quantities of guilt; and away from Corry, who'd begun to scare me several weeks into our physical intimacy.

After the first time we had sex, in her bedroom, she insisted that I meet her parents. They were downstairs. I suggested that I climb down from her balcony and ring the doorbell. She laughed and asked why I would do such a thing. I asked if she took a lot of guys to her bedroom and then introduced them to her parents immediately following sex, and she laughed again, said she'd only had sex one other time in her life, with her cousin when she was fourteen. She told me she loved me and wanted to have children with me. But first I should meet her parents.

I met them, and had no idea if they realized I'd just performed a sexual act with their child. I hadn't known they were home, so hadn't worried about Corry's noises.

Her mother was gorgeous, tall, much taller than Corry, three or four inches taller than her husband. She looked me in the eye, smiled, and asked if I'd like to eat something. I smelled of sex; her face was three feet from mine, and yes, I was hungry. She made me a ham sandwich and served it with potato chips, carrot strips, and a cold beer she didn't even ask if I wanted. She and Corry watched me eat, smiling and chattering. Corry's stepfather had black hair slicked and combed and thick black-rimmed glasses; he'd helped raise her since she was three and yet, I'd learn, he was daily reminded by both his wife and his daughter that he was not Corry's "real" father, even given that her biological father had deserted her, and this man at the table with us, reading a paper, had always adored her unconditionally.

Corry's stepfather grunted hello, forced a smile, asked a few perfunctory questions as he perused the *San Diego Union* sports page. He asked me what sports I liked. I told him I kept up with everything, pretty much, played football, basketball, baseball in high school, though one year I ran track instead of playing baseball. I'd run the 440 or quarter mile; my fastest time? Fifty-three something, so mediocre I'd never placed better than fourth even against the worst schools, but just fast enough to keep me on the team.

He asked me what's this he's heard about me teaching karate; Corry'd told him something. I explained that I'd gotten a second-degree black belt in Sasebo, Japan, when my stepfather was stationed there. I gave private lessons, and a couple of group lessons. I used to have a huge class on the Amphib Base, but it got too big and the money wasn't good enough. I babbled on about the sixty tournament fights I'd had in Japan, how I'd won forty-nine of them, and how I particularly excelled at the kata, and at breaking things with my hand.

I'd never been one to brag, not about karate, anyway, but I sat there eating the guy's food, drinking his beer, reeking of the sex I'd minutes earlier finished having with his seventeen-year-old daughter, and I just couldn't stand the idea of any silence. It was as though the noise I made would somehow cover up the smell of what Corry and I had done.

The pathologies in that family were creepy, not run-of-the-mill, and seemed to center primarily on Corry's mother. She was in her mid-thirties, a junior high school dropout who'd gone through beauty school when she was eighteen and Corry was an infant. Her first marriage ended when her nineteen-year-old husband ran off with another teenager. Corry's mother did hair, met her present husband when she was twenty. He staked her in her own little shop, but she blossomed into a truly gifted businessperson, and additional large shops accrued. I got the feeling she wanted me to have sex with her daughter, there in that nice house near the golf course; I got the feeling that she figured such a circumstance was preferable to Corry going out at all hours.

When I told Corry's mother that I was "between apartments," that I was "staying temporarily" in the Coronado Tea Garden and the "guest house" of a friend on Orange Avenue, that I would soon move out to the university area, or maybe to Hillcrest on the bus route to State, she very quickly offered that I should stay with them anytime I wished. She could make up the couch for me.

Corry's stepfather said nothing, and I did not look in his direction; I simply thanked her, and said that she was being too kind. Corry was excited; smiling hugely, and her mother seemed almost to swoon to have made the otherwise dyspeptic little beauty happy.

I fell into a pattern of sleeping at Corry's officially two nights a week,

Tuesdays and Thursdays, so I could catch a ride with Corry's mother to El Cajon Boulevard, where it was a straight shot, a fairly brief bus ride, or I'd hitch a ride to save bus fare, to my classes at State. Friday and Saturday nights I sneaked into Corry's room while her parents were out, usually at separate events, and stayed holed up there until just after dawn, when I'd shimmy down her balcony and off to the beach, the library, then Dirty Dan's to get stoned. I'd return to Corry's for dinner. I was keeping Corry fairly happy, so Corry's mother was solicitous. Corry's stepfather, who came home every night at around eleven stinking drunk from the Mexican Village, was just quiet, despairingly calm. Once, he shook me awake and asked in a whisper for me to leave Corry's bed. I did, and another word was never spoken about it, though I continued to sleep in her room most nights other than Tuesdays and Thursdays, with the door locked.

I finally had no choice but to tell Corry's mother that Corry was well into her fourth month. The beautician rolled her eyes, held her face in her hands, and mumbled something about taking care of it, not letting Corry's stepfather find out.

I was relieved. It happened fast. Then Corry was gone. She was sent to an aunt's in San Bernardino.

On many of the nights I actually slept on Corry's couch I had lucid dreams in which I could fly. I'd never before had, nor would after have, such dreams, only on that couch over a period of two or three months. I'd dream I was precisely where I lay, and that I could leave my body and float anywhere I pleased, and would take extended flights out of the house, once I realized I could, usually flying to the golf course, though sometimes to the beach behind the Hotel Del Coronado, the "Del."

I was incredulous in the midst of the dreams, couldn't believe how real it all seemed, how focused my thoughts were. I was not at all certain that I was dreaming, but thought perhaps I was leaving my body. I once pressed my dream face to the windowpane behind the couch and stared into the mesh of the screen; there was a dead fly on the sill and when I awoke midmorning I shot up to look and it was there; chills shuttled my spine. I don't believe I'd left my body; I don't believe there is an "I" other than my body. I'd probably seen that little carcass on another occasion and just forgotten. But for a moment that black speck was my link to Heaven.

I slept at Corry's for the last time the night I'd told her mother she was pregnant. Corry's stepfather stumbled in at eleven and I was already on the couch, staring at the ceiling. I saw his shadow pause to look at me; then he struggled to take his shoes off, almost falling on his face when he reached down to hook his fingers in them to carry them upstairs. He'd thought I was asleep and tried not to wake me. I wanted to weep, but at that time of my life wasn't able. I wanted to go to him and beg forgiveness, not just for my intrusion on his life, but for the world's massive intrusion upon his good, sick heart. I was prepared to speak for the world to that man and ask sincerely for forgiveness.

I dreamed my last flight, beyond the Del, beyond the beach, over the ocean. The moon was small on the darkness, but I could see the waves coming in one upon the next, and I felt the most thrilling sadness, and heard a beating, a steady thumping on the air. And for the first time I wondered how high I could go, but then realized that that wasn't the point.

Corry phoned me at the geedunk; I was excited and annoyed to hear her voice. She told me she wanted to see me, that I should come to San Bernardino.

I was already seeing several women casually, one somewhat frequently. I'd moved into an apartment with three other guys on University Avenue. I still worked at the geedunk on weekends.

I didn't want to see Corry; I wanted her to be a memory. But I couldn't untether from the passion, so said I'd come up. Especially now that she wasn't pregnant, I wanted, quite desperately, to have sex with her.

The first thing she did when we were alone was show me she was still making milk. She pulled her breast from her shirt and squeezed it to show me the glistening film it produced weeks after the abortion.

We dropped acid and went to a bar she'd heard about called the Sandpiper; it was one she could somehow get into with her poor fake ID. I'd turned twenty-one. It was a cowboy/biker bar, and the acid really kicked in as we danced to a spirited shit-kicking group.

Figured I could get into it, so tried. I didn't know how to dance to shit-kicking music; I didn't really know how to dance to any kind of music, and never understood how people could enjoy writhing among strangers. But I was game if Corry was, and this was her idea, so I danced pretty much the only way I knew how, a weird little shuffle step with a lot of subtle hand-jive, a kind of all-purpose dancing, I thought. I was wearing my best black shirt; my hair fanned out over my shoulder blades. I wore tight jeans and orange sneakers stained by my janitorial work at the geedunk. I was on acid, Mr. Natural, I think, dancing my silly dance to shit-kicking music I didn't understand in my soul the way everyone around me did. I was with an exotic-looking little beauty who was dolled up and poured into something black and tight and wearing high heels as red as her lipstick. We were fresh bait for trouble.

First his girlfriend knocked into Corry and started roughing her up. I was tripping, and at that phase of the trip when one cannot comprehend why the world can't just be a paradise of happy people. I yelled over the music that whatever had happened, Corry bumping the cowgirl, I figured, had been an accident, and then her boyfriend blindsided me.

The singer said something like, "Well, here we go again, folks," like this was no big deal, and later I'd realize that in that place's scheme of things it was indeed no big deal. I was tripping and some guy in a black leather jacket and a cowboy hat that flew off when he tackled me was literally growling in my ear. But at that moment, as I grasped for the guy's arms because he clearly wanted to pummel me, my single crystalline thought was what a goddamned chump I was to be on my back in a cowboy/biker bar in San Bernardino, California, the armpit of Western Civilization, tripping.

The guy was burly, much stronger than I, but I had powerful incentive to keep him from raising those strong arms from against his sides, so clasped him with an adrenaline-drenched will throwing off acid sparks throughout my body, and so the guy did something truly remarkable, something I shall always be in awe of; I looked him in the eye, nose to nose, thinking I'd reason with him, but before the words could form I saw the guy's face light up a little, as though he were suddenly suffused with enlightenment. The guy had an idea, a simple, pure, immediate course of action.

He opened his mouth, I thought to speak, and clamped down on my upper lip, taking a large chunk of it away. I gushed blood in his face and let him go, but as he rose from me, spitting a piece of me into the gloom of the dance floor, I popped him as I rose from my back, knocking him into the crowd surrounding us, but doing little damage. He hustled out the door.

"What the fuck happened to you?" Danny asked. His wetsuit was peeled down from his chest; he carried his board like he hardly knew he was carrying it.

I told him.

"Bummer," he said, and joined Roger and Stan. I watched from the rocks, smoking a joint gingerly, as he pointed back toward me, I assumed recounting the story I'd just told him about why I had fat stitches in my lip, why I was discolored there and just generally looked terrible. I'd even told him about the little Asian doctor named Li or Lu or Wang who sewed me up at 3 a.m., and how I'd caught the first bus out of San Bernardino. I didn't tell him, of course, that I'd never again see Corry, though I already knew I wouldn't. I couldn't know that in a few weeks she'd meet a Las Vegas card dealer and get married before the year was out, and, according to one of her girlfriends I'd run into a few years later, have three kids immediately.

He pointed back at me and the other surfers followed his gesture with their heads, their blond, beautiful heads, and I had to pinch myself around the stitches because I was laughing so hard. I was making the strangest noises because I was laughing uncontrollably but had to pinch my lip so I wouldn't burst the stitches, and the funnier I sounded to myself the harder I laughed, and tears poured from my eyes, and the surfers looked hard at me, and began to approach, wondering what I was doing, what was happening to me.

As they approached I became hysterical. I had to use both hands to hold my stitches and I was weeping with laughter, and I was making noises I'd never heard a human being make before, grunts wrapped in chortles, and as they got closer my laughter got more hysterical, because I could only guess from their expressions, which became clearer through my tears with each step they took toward me, how bizarre I seemed standing there on the rocks, holding my mouth with both hands, weeping, discolored, emitting an unearthly music.

THE CHINESE CONNECTION

FALL, 1974

I cannot think of Mao Tse Tung without envisioning very large breasts. If I were European, this would probably not be so, because the main way, no, the only way European culture is superior to American is that it does not make of female breasts altars at which to giggle insipidly. The American male gets giddy in the presence of large breasts, and Herman Melville understood why even if I don't.

Margaret Hicks was a Maoist. She always wore an apple-red beret that looked like something she'd have worn to her first day of school, and no matter how she cocked it on her brown hair it looked cute, and Margaret Hicks was the sworn enemy of all things cute, for cute was decadence, cute was bourgeois, cute was exploitation. The fact that Margaret Hicks was neither decadent nor bourgeois nor exploitative, and yet was so cute you wanted to pinch her cheeks and give her hugs every time you saw her wearing that apple-red beret tilted in her curly brown hair, seemed to annoy her, though not as much as the fact that everybody, even other women, stared at her breasts.

"Why do you do that?" she asked me. We rode the bus together from San Diego State, transferring once at Horton Plaza, back to Coronado.

"I can't help it," I moaned. "I try, Maggie, I really do. But they're huge. They're beautiful."

"You don't know that they're beautiful. They could be bags of shit for all you know. You've never seen me with my shirt off."

"May I?"

"I don't know. Maybe sometime."

"Maybe if I saw them raw I wouldn't stare at them when we talked."

"You think?"

"I'm not sure. Maybe."

Maggie hated the blue, arching Coronado Bridge, recalled the old "Nickel Snatcher" ferry of her childhood fondly. As the bus ground its gears ascending the arch, the bay, cluttered with sailboats and Navy transport vessels, glittered in the late afternoon sun.

"I hate sex," she breathed. She'd informed me of this weeks earlier.

"That's because you've only done it with dolts. You'll like it with me."

"They all say that. Especially the black guys."

"Yeah, well, for black guys bragging is foreplay."

"And obviously you're no different."

"I'm the heart of humility. That's why I'm such a good lay."

"There are children dying of hunger in Zimbabwe, and all you can think about…"

"Is precisely what their parents were thinking about," I interrupted, "even as other people's children were dying of hunger all around them."

It would go on like that down Third Avenue, past A and B to Orange Avenue, where the bus turned left after the light.

"I'm walking you home," I announced, following her off the bus at Seventh.

"Don't be an idiot. I don't need to be walked."

"I'm not doing it for you. I'm doing it for me."

"No one's home," she said.

"No one's ever home," I observed. "Maybe you'll let me come in this time."

"I'm not screwing you."

"Will you let me see your breasts?"

"Maybe," she said.

Her house was small; she was the only poor homeowner on the island, poor in the sense that she and her mother lived on a modest pension from the Navy as a result of her father's death in early sixties Vietnam, and on what her mother made in addition as a bookkeeper at Tenth Street Liquor, where Maggie herself worked one of the registers sometimes on weekends.

The place was a horror; it reminded me of how my mother, four brothers and sister and I lived in the projects, except it was much worse: clothes draping the furniture and clumped on the floor; the ammonia-laced odor of laundry spiraling the smell of the same four things cooked again and again; domestic filth not the result of benign neglect so much as a primal struggle. I knew immediately that two women who loathed each other lived in that house.

I could also see that one of them was a heavy drinker. Empty Smirnoff fifths were everywhere, on the couch, on the TV, knocked over on the floor, clustered on the kitchen table.

"Still want to do some sex?" she grinned, scooping up a boneless tabby from the kitchen counter. Some people can live like that and be blind to it, but she knew exactly its effect. She'd grown comfortable in it because eventually people grow comfortable in any circumstance that does not produce excruciating pain, but she was defiantly aware of how repulsive her house was.

"Sure," I chirped. "I just don't know where," I added, craning my neck to peek into a bedroom that was in unspeakable disarray, and from which the ammonia odor seemed strongest. Cat turds speckled the kitchen linoleum, so that was definitely out.

She cracked up, shaking her head. She boiled water, wiped out two beige mugs with a cruddy dishtowel and poured the water over Lipton bags.

I more or less cleared spaces at the kitchen table and sat across from her, the fingers of both my hands curled around the steaming mug.

"See, it's all in your head," she grinned. "You don't want to have sex with me now that you've seen this," she finished, sweeping her eyes across the room.

"That's ridiculous," I said, staring into my tea, and lying.

"When everything comes crashing down all domestic order will seem quaint," she said.

"Yeah, when the revolution comes, people will actually purchase dried cat turds to sprinkle on their floors," I speculated.

"Laugh all you want, son, it's coming."

"Freeze-dried cat turds?"

"And the funny guys will be the first to get shot against the wall," she smiled.

"When the revolution comes, will you shoot people?"

"You bet your ass. The first thing I'm going to do is take out everybody on this block over thirty." She wasn't smiling.

"You got a gun?"

"When the revolution comes, I'll get issued one."

"Maud Gonne," I blurted.

"What's that? German for 'My God'?"

"Yeah," I said, chuckling and not wanting to explain.

"Have you read *The Little Red Book*?" she asked in earnest.

"Snatches," I said. "I'm a Trotskyite," I announced, to myself as much as to her.

"Then you're scum."

"But I'm willing to reform."

"If you want to have sex with me you'll have to."

"Consider it done!" I said, staring at her breasts, oblivious to the squalor around us.

"Ain't that easy," she said. "You've got to read *The Little Red Book*, all of it, take it to heart."

"How will you know if I've taken it to heart?"

"You'll stop staring at my tits, for one thing," she said.

"Revolutionary peasants and the intellectual avant-garde have no interest in sex?" I wanted to know.

"The authentic revolutionary doesn't have sex in the head, and sees it as a means to an end."

"Orgasm?" I speculated.

"Procreation," she corrected.

"Ouch," I said. Then, "That sex in the head thing you keep saying. You know, D.H. Lawrence talked about that, and he was kind of a fascist, or at least he was no commie."

"Who's he?" she said. She'd told me before that *The Little Red Book* was the only one she'd ever read that wasn't about science.

She was a biology major, would become an RN to support herself until the revolution.

"A guy who saw himself as a kind of priest in the Church of Freud," I rattled much too glibly. But she was used to my glibness.

"Where *do* you live?" she asked, apropos of nothing.

"Right now, nowhere," I said, hoping to shock her, maybe even impress her.

"On the beach?" she wondered, deflating my confession a bit, for I was not quite so detached from bourgeois society that I could live on the beach.

"Yeah, well, sure, I've slept on the beach," I said matter-of-factly, but who hadn't at one time or another slept on the beach? I was lying a little, or misrepresenting my situation, so I added, "I stay mostly at the Coronado Tea Garden, sometimes in the guest house"—(a nasty shed)—"of one of my karate students. Two or three days a week I stay at my girlfriend's."

"That pretty little chick who came in with you on Friday?"

We'd stopped in at Tenth Street Liquor to pick up some beer; Maggie had been working the register. "Yeah, her," I admitted.

"She's got a rack," Maggie recalled.

"Yeah, but not like yours, Maggie, not like yours," I sighed.

"I wish I could get rid of them. Someday I will."

"That's stupid. They're a gift," I said.

"To you and to every other horny dude. To me they're just a burden. I mean literally. They make my back hurt."

"Are they why you're a Maoist?"

"Good question," she said, turning thoughtful, staring off. "Maybe they have something to do with it."

"What about your mother?"

"My mother's are small. I take after my father's mother."

"That's not what I meant. What does your mother think about the revolution?"

"My mother wants me to marry a doctor."

"That's normal," I suggested.

"Nothing's normal. She drinks herself to death and worries about my future."

"Maybe she's sad," I said.

"Sadness is a bourgeois state. Only the rich can afford to be sad."

"Maggie, your mother's hardly rich."

"It's relative. She lives in a rich community, owns her own home, never goes hungry, and can afford to buy as much alcohol as she wants. She's rich by comparison."

"Downtrodden peasants don't get sad?" I asked.

"They're in despair. That's something else," she said.

"You ever met any downtrodden peasants?" I wanted to know.

"I've seen poverty," she answered, averting her eyes.

"Yeah, well, I've *been* poverty. I've gone without eating for days. I've lived in places almost as nasty as this, and not because I wanted to. I've had people look at me in disgust and pity. And you know what?"

She blinked.

"The poor suck," I informed her. "I hate the poor. I mean, I really hate the rich, but I hate the poor, too."

"You'd live in a world of endless track homes and malls?" she asked sarcastically. "You long for a middle-class paradise?"

"No, the middle-class sucks, too," I admitted.

"Well, who does that leave?" she chuckled.

"Nobody," I admitted. "Everybody sucks as a member of a class, even revolutionaries."

"True revolutionaries identify with the peasants, but they're classless."

"Horseshit. They're a club. The same thing. The poor are a club. The middle-class is a club. The rich are just the top club, the really good one, so they suck the most."

"You're a fucking anarchist," she breathed, her nostrils flaring in disgust.

"No, they're a club, too," I said.

"Anarchists by definition can't be a club," she rolled her eyes. She was adorable when she rolled her eyes.

"Hey, they've got a name, right? Anarchist. You put an 's' on that and you've got a club. So they're an anti-club, but that still makes them a club. Anarchists are the most pathetic of them all."

"I thought you said the rich were," she said in a gotcha tone.

"No no no! I said they sucked the most. I didn't say they were pathetic. Winners can't be pathetic. They can be almost everything else that's bad, but not that."

"What's not a club?" she asked, dripping sarcasm.

"Two people screwing."

"What about three people?"

"Well, that's a club, a rather exclusive one, I'd say."

"Shit," she said, and rolled her eyes again, driving me crazy. "You're definitely going up against the wall, pal." She seemed sad to be breaking this news to me.

"Then you should show me your breasts," I insisted.

"Why?"

"Because I'm doomed, and it would be a nice gesture."

"Nice gestures are so bourgeois. But I'll tell you what."

"What?" I said, my pulse quickened by her sudden mischievous tone.

"I'll trade you."

"You want to look at something of mine?" I was a little thrilled to be asking.

"Yeah, in a way. I want to watch you do something."

Surely she could see me blushing even through my tan. This was too good. The squalor was becoming homey. Even the dried cat turds possessed a sudden, inexplicable charm. "Anything," I whispered.

She rose, turned, and took one step to the back door, opened it. "Come," she said. I stood and followed.

Her backyard, roughly fifty feet by seventy and enclosed by a seven-foot tall bamboo fence, was cropped and clean, uncluttered. Someone, perhaps both of them, worked diligently to keep it nice. A rose bush drooped with yellow blooms; a magnolia tree shaded two lawn chairs. The grass was clipped short and absolutely uniform, and an edger had been eased carefully along the borders of the cement patio.

"I want you to dance for me," she said, turning to face me. The sun was in her eyes. She raised her hand to shield her eyes.

"Say what?"

"I saw you one time in that karate suit with some surfers. You were teaching them a dance."

"A kata," I said.

"Yeah, whatever," she said. "I liked it. Dance like that for me and I'll show you my breasts."

"I don't get it," I said.

"It's kind of Chinese, right? That kind of dancing? Kata?"

"Well, not exactly, but kind of," I said, and felt silly; it was as Chinese as it was anything else. It was as Chinese as the language we were speaking was American, and British, and Australian.

"Just dance like that for me. Here. Right now. I really liked it when I saw you doing it. Like, about a month ago in the alley between Orange and C."

"Mr. Clean's," I said. Mr. Clean was what we called the swab who lived there and shaved his head and let me use his backyard to give lessons.

"I was walking through there from the bay. I had all my fishing gear, but I stopped and watched for a long time. I couldn't believe you were the same guy. You were beautiful."

I didn't want to look at her breasts. I didn't want to do a kata. I just wanted to leave. And I wanted to stand there. And I wanted to sit in one of the lawn chairs and watch the sun sag toward the ocean.

"Naked," she said. "I want you to dance like that naked. Do it naked and I'll do anything you want."

At the beginning of every kata, one presents one's empty hands, raised, then quickly turns them inward, concealing a fist with a "knife hand," though it is more a gesture of concealment than an effective act of stealth. The fist, symbol of overt power, is covered by the "knife hand," symbol of defense, and they are brought down slowly, the right index knuckle pivoting in the center of the left palm. Only when this symbol made with the hands has extended all the way down, covering the genitals for a moment, may the kata begin.

Poet, Ha Ha
Fall, 1974

Suzie Hitchcock was tiny; her blond hair was straight and perfect down to her tiny, perfect ass. We were in choir, she an alto I a baritone, and the group was arranged such that we sat next to one another. She deigned to speak to me because I was persistent and careful what I said. It was of course always I who initiated conversation between rehearsal sets; she volunteered nothing, which meant she thought I was too low class or simply too weird. The karate thing confused her, I could tell. She heard stories about me doing karate, that I'd earned a second-degree black belt in Sasebo, Japan where I'd attended eighth, ninth, and tenth grades, and now, a junior, gave private lessons even though I was only seventeen like her. She'd watched me break rocks at keg parties, and once I'd turned to glance at her after smashing one, and she'd looked mildly disgusted. She never volunteered anything about herself, but did from time to time ask questions. Where was I from? I couldn't give a straight answer because one didn't exist. Why had my name changed? Because I was adopted. Why was I adopted? I just didn't have time to go into it. I'd have told her if she'd ever agreed to meet me at the library, or at the Night & Day Café, or anywhere other than school. But there was always something she had to do after school and on weekends. Does it hurt when you hit them? No, not really, I lied.

I quit high school in the middle of my senior year; I went to L.A. to write songs with my best friend Bruce Donald for our mutual friend Robert Mancini. Bob had a record deal, and just had to acquire an album's worth of original material, of which he was short about half. I wrote lyrics, which any idiot can do and does; Bruce was, is, a brilliant composer and musician. He deserved better, but we both felt an odd loyalty to Bob, and really thought, at least I did because I had no taste, that Bob had potential to be a star. Bruce understood even then that any jerk with a double-digit I.Q. can be a star, so Bob certainly had a shot. Bruce also knew that stardom was a crapshoot and the dice were usually loaded.

I churned out hundreds and hundreds and hundreds of lyrics. They were almost always too literate or too much bitter parody of pop music:

> Thunder Woman two thousand pounds,
> Beatin' me up all around the town…
>> or
> The night you nailed me to the cross
> I moaned for love's salvation,
> But look out baby 'cause I ain't dead
> I'm having a rez-erection!

Bruce would chuckle and sigh when I handed him such drivel, and we'd both laugh about it, how all I could really do was just keep throwing shit against the wall until something stuck.

> You're just a one-night stand
> For a boy in a band
> Just one stop along the road,
> You're just a one-night stand
> For a guitar playin' man
> I gotta get back to the show

went the refrain to one that actually did stick; Bruce worked it up into a tasty little country-rock kind of number at a time when there really wasn't much of that sort of thing. Bob sang it like a cross between Jose Faliciano and Johnny Mathis, a vocal effect he reverted to when he didn't have a clue as to how to sell something. Bruce, his musical director for the album, was in despair.

Probably the best thing we wrote for Bob was something called "Sighing in the Night," which had been an experiment to see if I could write something absolutely void of meaning and possessing absolutely no emotional resonance. Bob took to it immediately.

To our great credit, none of us wanted to make "art" of Bob's album. We just wanted to get on the radio and make money. We possessed absolutely no artistic integrity, but then nor did we harbor any pretensions that we were doing something of real significance, or that art was even possible in popular music. Bruce was classically trained. I was, for my age, quite well read, especially in poetry and philosophy, and had thought of myself as a poet since the beginning of adolescence. Bob was simply an idiot, a guy with strong mathematical intelligence and incredible personal drive, but no emotional depth. He was a cartoon character who possessed a kind of mechanical talent but no soul, no soul whatsoever.

Bob's record deal went silly, but Bruce and I continued to write songs for him, though mainly we were doing it for ourselves, past a certain point. We'd get together intermittently and I'd bang out ditties, most of them wretched but not without charm; once in a while I'd nail a winner. It was only poor luck and lack of will that kept us from doing some significant work, significant, at least, from a pop music perspective. Our problem (mine more than Bruce's) was that we were condescending to the process even as we wished to be successful within it. I have seen dozens of concepts I had in the seventies turned into hits over the past three decades; of course, thousands of people were working the same concepts at the same time, which simply goes to show that concepts, like ideas, are cheap. The people who are the most successful pop songwriters believe, pathetically, that they are artists.

My dream was to knock out some hits and to live on royalties so I could do my "real" work. That I wasn't entirely sure who would read my "real" work, since even then it was fairly obvious that no one read "serious" poetry, deterred me not at all.

When I was eleven, living in the projects of Norfolk, Virginia, while my father was in prison, I one day decided to steal some books from a Salvation Army used-book sale in the parking lot of the Giant Open Air Market. I just walked by a table, grabbed two books and ran like hell. I was no thief, usually. I'd never enjoyed stealing. But I was bored; it was Saturday morning in autumn, a little chilly, exhilarating. I was feeling frisky.

One of those books was *Louis Untermeyer's Treasury of Great Poetry,* and the other was *The Complete Poems of Robert Frost.* I was eleven; masturbation had supplanted baseball as my favorite leisure-time activity. And there I stood, on the edge of what we called Hangman's Wood, an overgrown lot, really, clotted with trees, across the street from my little brick apartment in the federal housing projects that lay along the Elizabeth River, shaking my head in disbelief. What the hell was *this*? I wondered, leafing through the pages.

I read both books from cover to cover with little comprehension, and yet I knew that this stuff was like what I was trying to write about the mysteries of life, about the stars and where God sat among them. Robert Frost, especially, made a deep impression upon my adolescent emotional circuitry.

So a few years later I would sit for hours in the Coronado Public Library reading poetry and listening to records, in the sound booths, of Dylan Thomas and T.S. Eliot saying their own poems. One day, three skinny books lay on a table in the stacks: Philip Levine's *Not This Pig,* James Dickey's *The Helmet,* and James Wright's *St. Judas.* God knows who had left them out or how and why Coronado Public Library would have thought to have them on its shelves, but I spent days reading and rereading those books. *That's* what I wanted to do. A decade or so later, the publisher of all three would publish my first three books.

I wasn't shy about telling people I was a poet. I didn't make a big deal of it, but I didn't balk, either, at declaring myself that most rarefied of social beings. I didn't push poems under people's noses; I didn't recite my efforts to friends. I didn't even want to show anything I'd written to anyone I knew, especially not to anyone I knew; but I would tell people, when they asked me what I was doing, that I was working at the geedunk, giving private karate lessons, delivering pizzas for Joey's once in a while, taking some classes at City College and later at State, and writing and reading poems.

My buddies found it hilarious that I read and wrote poetry. It didn't jive with karate, or they thought it didn't, assuming it was something mostly for faggots and girls. I knew that it did jive, that poetry and karate had a lot in common. I wasn't able to say what that common ground was, but I knew it had something to do with the kata, the karate dances. And it just *did* jive with how one was supposed to act in the dojo in Japan, a certain easy seriousness people assumed there toward one another and what they were doing, a certain humble dignity before mysteries of life that one didn't yammer about, but always kept suspended just above one's head, out of sight but profoundly and unforgettably present. I'd gotten the same feeling reading Robert Frost's poems.

Suzie Hitchcock had transformed from tiny and adorable to voluptuous petite. She was just home from some expensive private university. I was much better looking than I'd been in high school, which seemed to piss her off more than anything. When I'd managed to creep and nudge into her proximity, and then cut her from the herd, she seemed enthusiastic to talk to me, but put out absolutely no positive vibe, certainly nothing sexual. She was a little in her cups, sloshing a glass of whiskey as she gesticulated, though spilling not a drop; she was practiced. She slurred in a way that made me want to dance her into a bedroom and ravish her against a door, and that was precisely my intention until about two minutes into the conversation.

Her attention was fixed on me as it had never been. She wanted, at that moment, to be nowhere else on the planet, doing nothing else, than talking to me at that party, swilling someone's liquor among former classmates and acquaintances, locked in a pointless verbal conflict with the dork she'd sat next to in high school choir.

Suzie wanted to tell me what she'd really thought of me in high school, what all her friends had thought of me. She was cocked and loaded for brutal honesty, and had me in her crosshairs.

"You look much better than you did then," she said, as though many years and not twenty-some months had passed. I told her she'd filled out nicely.

"Bet you get a lot of those girls at State to sleep with you," she said, and the operative phrase was "at State." I told her I wasn't lonely.

"Do you know what I though of you in high school?" she asked. I said that I did not.

"Would you like to know?" she teased, smiling coquettishly, a facial expression dripping irony. I told her not particularly.

She wasn't to be deterred. "I thought you were pathetic," she said triumphantly.

"Okay," I said.

"Do you want to know why?" I stared down at her placidly.

"Because you were so fucking conflicted," she slurred, surprising me a bit.

"How so?" I really wanted to know.

"That poetry thing," she said, sloshing her drink.

"I don't get it."

"You were this tough guy who did karate, and then you walked around telling people you were a poet, and then you won those poetry things." I'd won some prizes because only two or three other people had entered the competitions, but those victories had gotten well publicized for some reason. "Everyone thought, 'Karate Rick, Poet, Ha Ha!'"

"We're not going to have sex, are we?" I said.

She blushed, speechless. "No, we're not," I continued. "If you were the last twat on earth I wouldn't have sex with you. You're a mean-spirited little lush, and someday you're going to make a man exceedingly miserable."

Tears welled up in her eyes. I was suddenly infused with a bitter eloquence. "I'm a poet, goddamnit!" I'd said it loudly; others around heard me over the music, though probably hadn't quite made out what I'd said. "Someone like you could never know what that means. Because where a soul should go you've only got hollow attitude. You're AM radio, Suzy-Q."

She ran away; that is, she walked to the front door, put the glass down on a side table, opened the door and ran, literally, out.

I'd been a prick. I'd totally misread her. Or even if I hadn't, nothing she'd said deserved such a dressing down. She was little. Her posturing was toward a tall guy with a deep voice. It had taken some courage for her to address me that way. I ran after her.

As I caught up I told her I was sorry, that I'd been a prick. She kept walking, didn't look at me, but said that yes, I'd been a prick.

"Suzy, stop a minute, please."

We were on B Avenue, between 4th and 5th. The houses were nice. All the houses on Coronado were nice. Windows glowed; there were stars but no moon. I told her I was certain she had a soul, that it was simply different from mine. And I told her I admired her courage for talking to me that way, that it was hard for tall people to imagine what it's like always to be staring up at others, especially in crowds. I told her I was a phony, but there was no reason she should know that.

"What do you mean, you're a phony?" she asked without a slur. She'd sobered up.

"I just mean I'm not a tough guy, not really."

She stared at me for two beats, expressionless. Then she smirked and said, "You're fucking weird," and walked toward her car.

"So we're not going to have sex, right?" I shouted.

"Only in your dreams, Karate Poet," she shouted back without turning.

"Why'd you even bother?" I shouted.

She paused; her door was open. "Bother to do what?"

"Give me shit."

"Because you used to drool all over me."

"I still think you're hot. Will you have coffee with me? Smoke a joint?"

"I'm into chicks," she said, tilting her head and staring right into my eyes. From the distance of the street-breadth she didn't seem that small.

I was stunned, confused, delighted. "How are you into them?" I stupidly asked.

"The same way you are, Karate Poet."

It took a few seconds to register.

"I'm staying at my parents'. It's in the book. My girlfriend Macey came down with me. She didn't come to the party because she has a migraine. If you'd like to take both of us out to have coffee, give me a buzz," she smirked, and climbed in.

I made fists, put my feet together and bowed low to the car. In the dim light of a street lamp, as I slowly rose, I saw her laughing as she rolled away.

THE HEIST
FALL, 1973

"It'll be easy," Phil insisted. "I've already practiced jimmying the lock. Look all you got to do…" and he babbled and pantomimed slipping his knife in and just plucking the doohickey and holding the thingamajig with the knife while he took a piece of coat hanger and pushed the doohickey out of the slot. Piece of cake.

"The police station is half a block away, Phil," I said, as one might say, *You've got mustard on your sleeve.*

"Those piglets sit in the station scooping toe jam with a coke spoon." Phil had an original turn of mind, and it kept turning and turning.

"I'm in," said Barney, at first I thought inexplicably. He was much smarter than Phil. He was smarter than I. But he was desperate for money. He'd been losing at poker, was having a bad run for the first time in his life, and needed rent money. Since he was living in the apartment with me and the lease was in my name, I was heartened to see him taking some initiative. I just wasn't certain that stealing electric typewriters from Coronado High School was the most propitious manner in which to raise rent money.

"That's like, a felony or something," I observed.

"More than like it, partner," Barney grinned. He was warming to the adventure. He and Phil had been passing a roach at the kitchen table when I came in from a karate lesson I'd given to some zit-infested booger boy whose father had scheduled it.

"You know, guys, there are folks who do this sort of thing professionally. Phil, I don't care if you know how to manipulate doohickeys and thingamajigs like a regular Houdini. You don't really know squat about how to pull something like this off."

"True," Phil admitted, taking no offence, because he was unoffendable, and being so was one of his several unique gifts, none of which was tethered to anything like native intelligence. "But that's why we plan it out. I mean, I'm the big-idea guy, and you two are logistics."

"Give me a quick definition of logistics, Phil," I said.

"Fuck you," he said. He'd heard Barney say it before I got there.

"Looky here," Barney said. And I did, because I respected his opinion. "This ain't Chula Vista. This ain't Sweetwater. This ain't Mar Vista. This is Coronado. Nobody does this kind of thing here. Nobody breaks into high schools and steals electric typewriters. We'll cruise in and out like nothing. If cops spot us and ask what we're up to, we say we're transporting these fine machines to a warehouse under the bridge, and they'll want to know if we need any help. Jesus Christ, nobody we know has ever even thought of stealing! Not like this. It's a goddamned original idea!"

He was right. If we didn't act like thieves, no one could even conceive that we were thieving.

"So we steal how many?"

"We each carry two," Barney said.

"And then how do we convert these babies into cash?" This seemed to me a fairly important point.

"Hal Harrison will take all six off our hands, and pay six dime bags for each machine."

"And I'm supposed to put a line of coke on the counter at the Night & Day to get Trudy to make me a Three Egg Special?"

"It might work," Phil beamed. Barney sighed.

"I've already got 'em sold," he said. "Hal's shit is strong. We step on it once, and each of us walks with over two hundred bucks. Look, this whole thing takes like, twenty minutes. Two hundred bucks for twenty minutes of work. You ever got two hundred bucks for twenty minutes?"

Of course I hadn't. "Who's buying the coke?" I was curious.

Barney grinned. "Fred," he said.

"Fred what?"

"Spacey Fred," he specified.

I couldn't believe it. But then it all made sense. Spacey Fred had ODed on Dramamine. Spacey Fred had set up a deal to sell twenty kilos of Panama Red in Grand Forks, North Dakota, and I'd allowed myself to get sucked into the silliness of a road trip to Grand Forks with him, my karate student Tim, and the twenty kilos. Spacey Fred was famous for having bought a gram of powdered sugar, snorted it, and then gone back to purchase another gram. Spacey Fred had smoked many ounces of oregano for which he'd paid good money.

"Yeah, one time, my ass," I said to Barney. "You're going to sell Fred a little bit of coke and a lot of something else that's white, and then sell the rest of the coke." I knew I was reporting the future with absolute accuracy. In such matters, Barney was as predictable as heavenly bodies.

"So you were going to rip us off?" The light clicked on for Phil, who, if he'd saved the money he'd lost at poker to Barney, could have been driving a nice new van by then, and certainly would not have been so desperate for cash he'd feel compelled to practice the manipulation of doohickeys and thingamajigs with a pocketknife and piece of coat hanger.

"Okay, I'll give you guys three hundred apiece," Barney said, which meant he was going to make between six and eight.

"That's more like it," I said.

"Yeah," Phil agreed triumphantly.

"There's only one thing, guys," I said, sighing.

They blinked.

"I'm really bad at this sort of thing. My old man was a thief."

"That's cool," Phil said. He kind of knew the story; Barney knew more or less everything.

"Think of what you just said," Barney ordered. "You're really bad at this because your old man was a criminal. Where's the logic in that? The fact is you've got the genes to be really good at this sort of thing."

No, I told him, that would only be true if my father were a successful criminal. "Successful thieves are the ones who don't get caught. My old man's done, like, thirteen, fourteen years in federal prisons," I pointed out.

"Well, you got me there," Barney admitted. He was good at seeing other people's points of view. But then he brightened. "Then seize this opportunity," he said, "for redemption! You can do this one heist without fucking it up, and then stop while you're ahead. Your old man's problem was that he never stopped while he was ahead." There was a certain diabolical logic to Barney's formulation that I found attractive. As in all things, he was viewing life, in this instance my life, as a poker game. But I accepted the efficacy of his world-view, even as, over the years, I'd witnessed its limitations. Finally, it was the three hundred bucks, and the prospect of Barney paying back, in addition, the two months rent he owed me, that sealed our partnership.

Coronado High School was famously easy to break into. People broke into it sometimes to play volleyball on the commons, a broad space dusted with streetlight that seeped over the single-story roof, or simply for the thrill of screwing at school.

We discussed whether we should smoke a joint before breaking in. Phil argued that it would relax us, make the whole operation go smoothly. Barney straddled. He could see strong points on both sides of the issue. I asked Phil if he was out of his fucking mind, and told Barney he should know better.

I passed the roach to Phil and said, "Okay, we're in. Do we flip on the light? I mean, we don't want to stumble around for twenty minutes. You bringing a flashlight?"

Phil always held the smoke down a ridiculously long time. "Jesus Christ, Phil, you got a flashlight?"

He peered at Barney, bug-eyed from holding the smoke, turning red. He was asking with his eyes, *You got one*?

"Of course I've got a fucking flashlight," Barney answered Phil's bug eyes. Phil choked out the smoke and passed the clip to Barney.

"You ever hefted one of those IBM's?" I asked them.

Barney toked, stared down, considering. Phil looked puzzled. "Yeah, I get your point," Barney said.

"What point?" Phil asked.

"They're pretty heavy, Phil," Barney said.

"Look guys," I began, taking a short toke off the roach and passing it to Phil who practically ate it, "just try to visualize. You've got a bulky forty-pound machine under each arm. You have to trot to the fence. You have to put down both machines without fucking them up. Now if you were carrying just one it would be easy, but you've got two. Imagine putting them down on the cement." I paused while they imagined. "Pretty tricky, huh? But then after we've put all six forty-pound electric typewriters down, someone's got to climb the fence, drop to the other side, and then we've got to get all six forty-pound machines over the fence to that person. Who's it going to be?"

"Me," Barney said.

"Okay, fine, but you see how it's a good idea to get these kinds of details nailed down now rather than on the spot," I said, firing up the nub of the roach with my lighter and sucking the smoke through my nose.

"What'd I tell you about genes?" Barney smiled. "You're a fucking natural!"

The compliment depressed me. I didn't want to be a successful criminal, but I wanted to be an unsuccessful one even less. "I've only defined the problems," I said. "I haven't solved them."

"Yeah, well, here's the deal," Barney said, taking charge, as it was inevitable he would do. "When we get in, you'll pick the machines. You'll be the only one who goes into the room after Phil gets the door open. You grab one, run to the door, give it to Phil. Phil passes it to me and I run and put it down at the fence. When we've got all six out…shit, get eight or nine! I'll jump the fence. Phil can stand on the bar in the middle, and you can pass the machines up to him and he can pass them to me. I can grab one, then just jump down put it down, and get back up again until we've got them all over. Then you guys'll climb over, and we'll just hustle 'em into the car."

"Fine. Sounds good. But whose car?"

"Oh, let me see," Barney said in a doofus voice, "how about the only guy I know who actually drives a station wagon." Phil smirked. I was forever catching goof for owning a station wagon.

"I hear the chicks get wet whenever they see you tooling around in that boat," Phil said for maybe the eightieth time.

I loved my '67 Mercury station wagon. It was perhaps the most wretched machine ever to roll out of the factories of Detroit, but it was mine.

"Then I want more money," I announced. Barney shook his head in appreciation, not agreement. It was as though all that he'd tried to teach me was finally sinking in.

"Fifty bucks," he said in a tone signaling that that was it, so I said nothing and thereby accepted.

"Okay, say we get all the machines into the back of my car. Then what?"

We take them directly to Hal's," Barney said. That wasn't so bad; Hal lived five blocks from the school, east toward the golf course. Hal lived in a house that was almost a mansion with parents and seven siblings; he was the oldest of the Harrison brood. Hal's father was a captain and Hal was a simi-big-time coke dealer who had a ham radio in his basement; he spent hours underground chattering to other ham-radio geeks in places like Borneo and Jakarta, and otherwise running his tiny but aggressively expanding coke empire. I preferred the idea of taking them there directly rather than hiding them in Phil's garage or, worse, taking them back to the apartment. There was no bullshit with Hal.

I wore black pants and a black tee shirt; Barney wore a dark-blue Hawaiian shirt and black sweat pants. Phil wore white shorts and a screaming pink tee-shirt that had white palm-tree silhouettes all over it.

"I've got an idea. Why don't you just stroll over to the fucking police station and turn yourself in right now, Phil," I suggested, then explained to him, slowly, why it was a good idea to wear dark clothes on such an occasion. Barney loaned him dark pants and a dark shirt.

Driving three blocks to the school was easy. Parking on the south side of the building, the side not visible to anyone coming out of the police station, was easy. Walking to the fence, climbing over it, was easy. Hustling to the typing classroom was easy. Getting the door open by way of Phil's hard-won skill at doohickey and thingamajig manipulation proved not at all a simple task. No matter how Barney held the light, it wasn't enough for Phil to work his magic with the pocketknife and four-inch piece of coat hanger. He diddled and diddled, cursing and sighing, until I told him to move out of the way and kicked at the door in the vicinity of the lock five times as hard as I could. The door opened out, so there was no way I could kick it open, but I figured I could loosen stuff up a little. The lock broke.

We nabbed seven, half of what were in the room, exactly as Barney had planned. They were even more cumbersome and heavy than we'd imagined, but we huffed and grunted and cursed them over the fence no problem, then into the back of my '67 Mercury station wagon.

Then, driving over to Hal's, a massive guilt descended upon me. I saw my father counting out a thousand dollars in small bills onto one of the twin beds in a Holiday Inn. He was drunk and had just ordered a large amount of fried shrimp because that was my mother's favorite food. The younger kids giggled as he counted out the money loudly, with that smile he only showed when he was drunk; he never smiled when he was sober, and hardly stopped when he was drunk. And now he was performing for his family, standing at the foot of a bed with a wad of cash in one hand, wearing only his drawers, peeling bill after bill with the other hand and slamming it on the pile with a flourish, yelling the tally with each bill.

He'd been out of prison for a few weeks. This was our second Bad-Check Tour of America. I was old enough to know that he'd not been "away at school learning a trade" for three years. I knew he'd stolen that money he was now playing with, that the shrimp my mother and the rest of us were devouring had been purchased with stolen money. I'd begun to weep and Dick couldn't understand why, so he beat me savagely for crying like a girl.

I pulled the car over. I said I couldn't do it. If Barney couldn't make rent in a week, we'd get evicted, and I didn't have anything remotely lined up to move into, but I couldn't do this. I told my friends to get out of the car. It was past midnight; the air was warm, breezy, perfect. They protested, Phil screaming that I was a pussy, Barney yelling that I was mental, that he'd always known I was out of my fucking mind. I told them to get out of the car or I was going to jack them up. They were scared of me, so they got out.

"What you going to do with them?" Barney yelled from outside the car. All the windows were down. I told him I was taking them back. Phil kept muttering about pussy as he crammed his hands into Barney's pockets and walked away.

I stacked them by the fence, in a patch of shadow. I had tears in my eyes, but I wasn't weeping. I wouldn't be able to weep for many years. My silent tears were the issue of guilt. I was hurting my friends. Barney needed the money. He and Phil had trusted me. I hated that school, had quit it as soon as I could. It didn't need these machines; the school could buy new ones, probably intended to, anyway.

But I couldn't do it. Phil was right, and I was ashamed that I couldn't rip off IBM typewriters from Coronado High School. Barney and Phil would tell everyone what I'd done, and the guys they'd tell would smirk but say nothing because they'd be afraid I'd pound them into dust if they said anything about my being such a pussy.

After my father had beaten me he'd put the thousand dollars in a drawer, said that was just the beginning, that he was going to get more tomorrow and the day after that we were flying to Hawaii. And he did, and we did, and on the plane I sat next to him. I was ten and scared. I somehow knew that he was crazy, that how we were living wasn't right. I asked him how he got the money. He kept his eyes closed and said, "Ricky, Ricky, Ricky," but that's all. He wouldn't answer; I asked again and he said, "Ricky, Ricky, Ricky," and took my hand, and I was heartened by such a gesture of affection, but he slowly began to squeeze it until his holding my hand was not an act of affection but of punishment, and I knew that if I cried he'd crush my hand so I wept without sobbing in his grip.

I'd stolen food when I was desperately hungry, and once or twice when I wasn't. In Elizabeth City, I'd discovered that very early in the morning I could skim with a flat stick under the door of the drug store downtown and slide out nickel's, dimes, even some quarters, the change that had been left by the magazine delivery man. At that same store, and later in Norfolk at the one near my end of the projects, I'd put one comic book inside another and pay only for the one. I'd taken money out of my mother's purse a few times, but had given her so much of what I'd earned doing odd jobs in the neighborhood, I'd not felt too bad about taking back a little. When I was fourteen I'd stolen from my new stepmother quite a bit of the government-issue funny money military guys and their families used on the base in Sasebo, Japan; that was the worst thing I'd ever done, and my doing it had had something to do with my confusion as to who I was and who and what I'd been just a few months earlier. It'd also had something to do with my first non-onanistic sexual experience, with a prostitute, and the fact that I'd liked it a lot. And of course over the last couple of months I'd ripped off dozens of sailors delivering pizzas for Joey's.

When I did the kata, I stepped into a nobility few may have purchase on, except that they enter a formality constructed of the ideal of nobility. I didn't understand that, and of course my life was anything but noble; it was indeed goofy almost to cosmic proportions. But I had a nobility I could enter, occupy for a while, something my young-man's body could adhere to that wasn't tainted by the spunk of lust, something ancient and spiritually dry, a place where the absence that is God gazed upon me not to judge but to admire.

I stood on the rock behind the Hotel Del Coronado, the flat granite platform facing the dark and mulling waves of the Pacific. I threw punches, kicks. I practiced my combinations. I knew that if anyone saw me they'd think I was nuts, or just silly, and I was of course exceedingly silly, but I needed to be serious about life for a little while, and that was the only way I knew how.

Business
Spring, 1974

If I'd had any business sense I could have made a decent living teaching karate, and wouldn't have had to swab floors at the Amphibious Base geedunk and hustle pizzas for Joey's. But after a certain point, after I'd been teaching someone for a while, I felt weird taking money from him. I conceived of money exchanged for services as something that had to remain impersonal, and once I'd gotten to know someone I couldn't pretend that our relationship was that way. I didn't just show up and start barking at a student, or at two or three or four if it were a group lesson. We'd shoot the breeze first, sometimes after a lesson smoke a joint. I gave good, solid, professional instruction and charged less than half of what I should have, and still had a hard time reminding guys to pay me.

"You're a chump," Barney told me, but I knew I was and didn't appreciate his rubbing it in. "You need a manager," he added.

"I need a rich uncle. I need a sugar mama. I need five bucks," I replied.

"How many students you got?" Barney asked.

"I don't know, maybe..."

"Bingo, you can't even say off the top of your head how many customers you've got."

Customers made me wince.

"Yeah, chump, they're your customers," Barney said. "You've got to put your heart on ice, chump. Business is business is business, and if you ever get to heaven and peek under God's robe, where the rest of us got a pecker He's got business."

Barney was tripping, so I didn't argue that even if there was a heaven and I someday stood before the Almighty, I'd not likely be inclined to lift the hem of His robe. "When d'you start coming on?" I asked.

"I don't know, sometime towards the end of the last Ice Age," he replied.

"Good shit?"

"Clean," he said, and closed his eyes and let his head fall back against the wall. "I'll be your manager, chump," he said without opening his eyes.

"You call me chump one more time, and I'll really start fucking with your head," I threatened.

"You can't fuck with my head," Barney chuckled, and I knew he was right. I could kick his ass, but I couldn't fuck with his head. And I'd never have thought to jack him up.

"What is it? Mr. Natural?"

"It ain't nothing like that," he said as Odysseus may have commented upon his visit to Hades. I was reading Edith Hamilton.

"Orange Barrel?" I wondered.

"NoNoNoNoNo…" he breathed, his eyes closed, his head against the wall.

"So?" I said.

"It ain't got a name yet," he breathed. "It's the pure shit," he added. "Rocky got eight tabs from Rodger."

Rodger was finishing a Ph.D. in Chemistry at UCSD. Rodger actually made it from scratch. I was impressed. "Let's do some math," he said without opening his eyes.

"For fun?" I said.

"For profit, asshole," he said, his body, even his face absolutely still except when his lips moved. He was an oracle. And he was the only person on the planet with implicit permission to call me asshole.

"Ok, Barney, I'll do math with you."

"How much you charge?"

"I don't know, some guys fifteen a month, most of them ten."

"You're a bigger chump than I thought. How many students you got? Concentrate, chump."

"There are over twenty, but, you know, guys come and go. They'll flake out for a couple of weeks, a month, then come back loaded for bear."

"Fuck 'em. They sign up they pay, whether they do it or not."

"Sounds cold," I said.

"Business," Barney breathed.

"How you going to make them?"

"Contract. A written agreement. You got anything in writing with these dudes?"

"Why would I?" I asked too earnestly.

"Business," Barney said. "You think you could get more students?" He was shadowed in the late-afternoon light as it slanted over the couch, his arms out Jesus-style across the breadth of the coach, his face tilted up. He was giving me the creeps.

"Yeah, sure, guys are always asking."

"A lot more?"

"I don't know, a dozen at least," I answered.

"Okay. Say you got thirty-five students total. Say you charge each forty bucks a month."

"Holy moly, Barn, that's a ton. I can't charge that much."

"If you charged that much, people would take you more seriously. You'd be beating off prospective students with a stick. A lot of old dudes, guys in their thirties, would want to work with you. Forty times thirty-five is one thousand four hundred. A month, chump. I take, say, six hundred, and you're left with eight hundred a month. Could you live on that?"

"Like a fucking king, Barney, but things never go down that smoothly."

"You let me handle the business, and just teach karate. In a year we'll be grossing sixty grand every circle of the sun, and almost half of that will be all yours."

"I'll never make that much money in my whole life. Stop putting such thoughts into my pretty little head."

"In five years, we can start selling franchises, like that dude that's got 'em all over the place. You checked him out at his place in Chula Vista."

Chuck Norris. I'd sat in to watch him test a guy for black belt. He was incredible, and his students were damned good. "Now this is the acid talking," I mumbled.

"Say we start opening 'em up in this region, and move east, into Arizona, New Mexico, Texas, then we skip all that garbage in the middle and hit Atlanta, work down into Florida, then back up the eastern seaboard. We're looking at roughly a net profit of between two and a half and three million a year. We rent spaces in tony neighborhoods. Stick to the upper-middleclass clientele. That's our niche. Of course we'll have to buy a lot of insurance…"

He didn't move anything but his lips. "You got five bucks, Barn? You owe me three hundred and eight."

"I'll just subtract it from my first month's pay," he said.

"I'm hungry. I need five bucks."

"I'll pay you with interest. Take it out of my cut."

"There's not going to be any cut. You're going to come down in about twelve hours and won't remember any of this."

"I never forget business," he said.

"This is talk, not business."

"It's thinking like that'll keep you poor, chump. Good thing you got me. Business is all talk."

"Then you're all business."

"Damn right," he said, splayed out for all the world like Christ lounging through the crucifixion.

"Then how come you owe me three hundred and eight dollars? You're down over a grand, Barney, with no job and no prospects for one."

"I just created a job. We're going to make millions. That's how it's done. And every entrepreneur is in debt up to his ass. You can't officially call yourself on entrepreneur unless you're in hock."

"So you don't have five bucks?" I whined.

"I've got millions, but they're tied up in an idea. And you're the instrument of my wealth."

"Well I'm really fucking glad to be of use, but man I'm starved."

"You work three jobs. How can you be broke?"

"Well, first of all, I'm carrying your ass."

"Not very far."

"Far enough to be broke. Look, I'll make a deal with you." Hearing "deal" Barney actually stirred. He twitched his head. "You give me five bucks, I'll pay you back five thousand once we've got all those franchises on the eastern seaboard."

"You'll put that in writing?" Barney asked.

I went to the kitchen table. There was a yellow pad. I got a pen from the fourth drawer down by the fridge. As I wrote I announced what I was writing: "If he gives me five dollars right now, I promise to give Barney Ward five thousand dollars after he has made us both rich in five years."

"Better make it seven," Barney said.

"I thought you said five."

"I'm playing it safe," he said

So I marked out five and wrote, "Seven," I said. "Now give me five bucks."

"Sign it," he said.

"Oh, yeah," I said, and signed my name.

"Date it," he ordered.

"Yeah, sure," I said, and did. "Five bucks," I chirped.

"Look in the closet. Where I keep my pole and stuff."

I opened the door to the closet. There was his fishing pole. His tackle box. "Okay," I said.

"Open my tackle box."

I stooped to his green aluminum tackle box, flipping the latches, lifting the top. Hooks, the stink of bait, tangled fiberglass line, several condoms. "Hey, Barney, what you do with those fish after you catch them?"

"Eat 'em, chump."

"Doesn't look like that's all you're doing to them. Where's the money?"

"Lift out the top drawer," he instructed.

I did. More tangled line, rusted hooks, slivers of shrimp shell, and a rolled up *Twat*, its pages filled with the scankiest beavers, spreading joyfully to earn the mag's moniker. I leafed through it quickly. "No money here, Barn."

"There's a film case."

Everybody used the gray plastic film cases to carry drugs. I saw two. One had an "F" felt-penned on its side. "One's got an F," I said.

"Other one."

I opened it. A key.

"It's a key, Barn."

"Go to the bedroom."

I walked into the bedroom.

"Yeah?" I said.

"Third drawer."

I opened it. A metal box. I unlocked it with the key. Pesos. No dollars. About two hundred pasos. "Goddamned pasos, Barney! Goddamnit!"

"And it's all yours, pal," he breathed.

"How the hell am I supposed to buy something to eat with this?"

"I recommend that you drive south about ten miles," he said.

"Barney, I'm coming over there in one minute and rifle through your goddamned pockets. I'm going to yank your wallet and take everything I find. Then I'm going to break every goddamned window in your car. Then I'm going to call Brenda and tell her you weep her name in your sleep. That she'll have to come over here to take care of you because you're trying to kill yourself with drugs you love her so goddamned much." Brenda had been crazy over Barney for years. She was extremely unattractive and not very bright, and Barney made the mistake of having sex with her once. She got pregnant but miscarried. She was very aggressive, stalking him periodically. I knew that he was deeply frightened of her.

He didn't respond. Didn't move. He was formulating. He was in another galaxy, processing what he was hearing from this one. Processing, formulating.

"The freezer," he said. I went to the kitchen, opened the freezer.

"Okay, I'm in," I yelled.

"Reach all the way to the back," he said. I did. Nothing. And then I felt something under a package of freezer-burned hamburger that had been there when we moved in. A lime-green change purse. Eight dollars and forty-seven cents. I took five dollars and put the purse back. Then I pulled it out again and took the rest.

"You need anything?" I said before I closed the door behind me.

"Beer. Lots of beer."

"I don't have enough for that," I said.

"Here," he said, and pulled some bills out of his pocket without opening his eyes. The room was dusky. I didn't flip on the light because I knew he probably needed to sit in the dark. I took the six or seven crinkled dollar bills.

At the A&P I bought three quarts of Coors, a large bag of rice, two large red onions, some garlic, pasta, tomatoes, two cans of tuna, eggs, bacon, a jar of chunky Skippy, some chicken thighs, and a loaf of bread. With the money left over, I'd get a Three Egger at the Night & Day after midnight and still have bus fare to make it to class at State tomorrow.

I opened a quart for Barney and handed it to him. He drained it. I opened another for him and the other for myself. I immediately slabbed some Skippy on a piece of bread to take the edge off. I stuffed it in my mouth then walked into the living room and asked Barney if he wanted some spaghetti. He turned his head to look at me, a puzzled, troubled look on his face.

"What?" he said.

"Yowasospetti?"

"What?" His eyes were huge with fear. My cheeks were packed with the sandwich and he couldn't understand me through the peanut butter. I must, at that moment, appearing from the light of the kitchen, my cheeks stuffed, garbling words, have freaked him out. I realized what had happened, that I'd frightened him, that he was hallucinating God-knows-what, so I chewed a long time as he stared in fear, swallowed. "It was just peanut butter, Barney. Calm down."

"I'm calm. It's just that I can't feel my dick."

"Okay," I said. "But maybe that's just nature's way of telling you to leave it alone when you're tripping on acid."

"Yeah, nature," he mumbled, staring off.

"You want some spaghetti?"

"What do you mean do I want some?"

"Barney, I'm going to boil some spaghetti. I'm going to make some sauce out of onions, garlic, olive oil, and smashed up fresh tomatoes and bacon. I'm going to season the sauce with rosemary and basil and salt and pepper. I'm going to toast some bread in the oven with margarine and diced up garlic on it. Then when I've got everything prepared, I'm going to smoke a joint, then sit down at this table and eat. Do you want to eat some of this food I'm preparing?"

"I don't think I can get off this couch," he said.

"I'll bring you your plate," I said.

"It'll just turn to shit," he said in all seriousness.

"Yes, Barney, that is exactly what it will do. Your body will do its job. You'll eat the spaghetti and the garlic bread, and it will pass through you. Your body will get what it needs, and some of what it doesn't, and turn everything else into shit."

I thought I heard him mumble, "Business," but wasn't sure.

"What you say?" I asked. But he was zoning out. There was no way he could eat anything, at least for another three or four hours, but that was precisely what he needed to do. I'd later smoke some joints with him, try to take some of the edge off. I'd make him some toast, and I'd try to get him to eat some of the spaghetti I'd save for him. I'd hang out and try to talk him down a little. He had a tough mind; he'd pull out of this. Though he was definitely fucked up beyond anywhere I'd ever seen him. He was deep inside himself, where advantage got hefted, where his portion of the world was forever being negotiated, where sanity, loving kindness, loss and revenge played hand after hand of five-card draw, and where his dead mother sat behind translucent glass, chatting with mine.

CAMERON CROWE'S MOTHER
SPRING, 1973

In the movie, she was a "professor." At San Diego City College she was actually a counselor, though maybe she also did some teaching and therefore deserved the moniker. I visited her office twice, as I recall, once to cheat the science requirement, once to cheat the math requirement. She didn't allow me to cheat either, though she cut me some bureaucratic slack, for which I was truly grateful.

Cameron and I hung out on campus. We were in a Greek Mythology class that he pretty much slouched through inattentively, perhaps knowing in his barely eighteen-year-old heart that he would someday be wildly successful and famous, and therefore would not need that crap, except for a few things, broad categories, psychological scaffolding, archetypes to proceed from when he would make movies in Hollywood in twenty, thirty years. He was smitten with Louanna, the woman I was living with, and called me a swine because I got to have sex with her. I'd smile deferentially when he called me that, though towards the end of the semester I'd gladly have traded my gorgeous, half-heartedly suicidal sex partner for his mother, as bizarre as such an exchange is to contemplate. That is, I'd have gladly exchanged wild sex for mother love, for such comfort. I was scared and emotionally unbalanced, and the only therapy I had purchase on were the kata, the karate dances I performed everyday as a physical regimen, but mainly to calm down, get centered. I also smashed bricks and rocks, but that was mainly to hurt myself, inflict a little manageable pain upon myself, to channel a rage I felt for my dying mother, a rage that was despair, despair that simply couldn't present itself as such to a self-involved boy-man. She was dying and I didn't know where, and thought that I didn't want to know. She'd started dying of multiple sclerosis six years earlier, before I was adopted and moved to Sasebo.

At first, I tried to forget her because I had little choice, being so far away. Then, I tried to recall her and simply couldn't, and I was enraged that I couldn't conjure her face, couldn't recall the precise tenor of her voice. I blamed her for allowing me to be adopted, allowing me to desert her. Afternoons, home from classes, I smashed bricks to exorcise rage and then did kata to feel peace for a few minutes.

Cameron had already done numerous covers for *Rolling Stone*. He was in the process of pretty much making some band's career with another cover story, I think it was Yes, but I can't recall and refuse to look it up. And yet he was incredibly humble about it, or, rather, unaffected; he had a gift for talking about his accomplishments without seeming to brag, and would only talk about his rock and roll journalism when I pressed him. He was a sincere, skinny, goofy looking kid. He hooked his long, straight brown hair behind his ears. He looked exactly like his mother in the face, which was long and kind of flat; there seemed quite a distance between their eyes and their mouths, but that flat, elongated look was not unpleasant on either of them, and it was especially striking on his mother when she smiled.

Which I remember her doing the day she introduced, at some sort of assembly she'd organized, a woman who claimed to be a psychic, and whose specialty was auras. The psychic said that everybody's got one, and that by learning to see them we may manage our lives better, relate more soulfully with fellow living beings, including plants; improve our health, and other such horseshit.

And though I thought it absurd, I was deeply attracted to the idea, to the whole paranormal shtick, and was attracted to how unabashedly Cameron's mother embraced and promoted it seemingly in every aspect: auras, out-of-body travel, talking to the dead. There was no one dead yet with whom I wished to shoot the breeze, though, like anyone, I fancied an Afterlife, and what was nice about how Cameron's mother seemed to conceive such a realm was that it didn't glitter beyond the Distance on the Look of Death, but was all tangled up in some wacky, cosmic fashion with lived life, each moment. The dead were always happily chattering at us if we'd only learn to hear.

She was sane, funny, personable, decent, and she obviously loved her job. She was roundly liked, respected, and even the most skeptical among us admired the enthusiasm with which she embraced that particular world view, and everyone seemed to want to go there, to that place of enthusiastic acceptance of an active realm of the spirit, a place where one "learned" to see auras, read minds, fly through the ether while sleeping, chat with the dead.

Cameron invited me to go with him on his interview of Robert Plant and Jimmy Page while they were in San Diego, and like an idiot I didn't take him up, nor did it really register what an interesting opportunity he was casually offering me until a few years later.

I was never star-struck or in any sense enamored of famous people, especially rock stars who I even early on felt to be dolts. I didn't yet conceive clearly of a bifurcation between "popular" culture and all that other stuff, like Shakespeare and Beethoven and Michelangelo, but besides Mythology and a Brit. Lit. Survey and Modern Drama and Astronomy (which I hardly ever attended), I was taking a Shakespeare course from Dr. Barnake, who told us the Secret of Life before we'd even read a single line of Shakespeare: "You want to know the Secret of Life?" he asked us, in a good-humored though conspiratorial tone, as though he were about to leak classified information. We leaned forward, tilted our heads just a little closer to his. "Everything comes down to two things, fighting and fucking. That's the Secret of Life, and no one illustrated it better than Shakespeare." Then we spent the entire semester reading two plays aloud in class, taking turns reading the various parts. He more or less explained every line that needed explaining; we lingered over soliloquies. One of the plays was *Merchant of Venice*, and Barnake spent a lot of time talking about Shylock from his own very New York Jewish perspective. He was old and would die in a few years, and if he'd been much of a Shakespeare scholar he wouldn't have been schlepping at San Diego City College, and of course his "close reading" of two plays was just plain laziness, his getting over, and yet it turned out to be a deeply valuable experience, more so than if he'd been a truly responsible professional and compelled us to read at least six plays, and lectured on historical context and received academic wisdom. Whether he meant to or not, he taught us something about bringing our lives to literature, to art. Besides, armed with the Secret of Life, we were from that point forward protected from all claims of intellectual authority, of special, secret knowledge, secret in the sense that such knowledge may seem cloaked in an obfuscating complexity. No matter how complex a human construct may seem, it could always be boiled down to the same two things.

And of course this was no less true for popular or commercial art than for that other stuff that got talked about in classes. So, one day as I sat in the cafeteria witnessing a friendly, caffeine-fueled argument between two Vietnam vets, I was smug in my two-thing wisdom. The argument was over whether Jimi Hendrix was a major artist.

The guys I was swilling coffee with and whose argument I enjoyed were six or seven years older than I, and both had spent a lot of time in the "bush" in "Nam." They both wore their hair long and were going to City College on the G.I. Bill. They were philosophy majors, and worked a lot therefore with Dr. Young, the only philosophy instructor at the college, a heavy-featured completely bald white guy who played the role of philosopher to the hilt. He wore a shirt and tie but sat on his desk full-lotus when he lectured.

"Hendrix was a damned good guitar player, within a narrow range, but rock and roll ain't art, therefore you can't, at least shouldn't, call him a major artist," Ned asserted.

The other vet, Hugh, laughed contemptuously. "What the fuck do you mean rock and roll's not an art form? Anything can be an art form if it's done artfully!"

"You're saying everything can be done artfully?" Ned asked.

"Okay, no, mass murder can't be done artfully," Hugh said.

"Well, you start out with the bar pretty high, there, bro," Ned chuckled.

"Okay, shitting can't be done artfully. Nor can bathing, for example, unless either activity were done before a discerning audience willing to compare particular performances to many, many others."

"Well, maybe you're confusing art and sport with that analogy, but if I'm hearing you right you're saying art is an issue of audience?" Ned asked in a tone of mock innocence, like someone setting a trap.

"Yes, of course, it's partly an issue of audience," Hugh replied like someone who knew he'd just stepped onto a slippery slope.

"So something's not art unless it's perceived as such?" Ned grinned.

"Kiss my ass. I'm not falling for that. But yes, damnit," Hugh said, flustered but defiant, "I've got eight minutes before I've gotta listen to some geek drone about isomers, so I don't want to get into that intentionality bullshit, or into some if-a-fucking-Greek-vase-shatters-in-the-forest-and-nobody's-there-to-hear-it Bishop Berkeley bullshit, but yeah, if a bunch of people are made happy by something, are moved by it, are uplifted or made thoughtful, then the goddamn thing walks like a duck, looks like a duck, and sure as hell sounds like a duck."

"Yeah, but does it taste like a duck?" I interjected, desperate to participate in this heady conversation. Both of them looked at me, then shook their heads and chuckled. Yet again, I'd said something really stupid. But they were patient with me, liked me for some reason. "Come on, guys," I said, flailing to save my rhetorical ass, "we're talking appearance and reality. A counterfeit mallard would not likely be as succulent as the real thing!"

"No, little bro, you're probably right," Hugh said, staring into his coffee. He was black, had an enormous 'fro, two Purple Hearts he'd mentioned once in passing as one might mention high-priced dental work.

"No, but seriously," Ned said, trying to get some momentum back before Hugh had to head off to class, "I'll allow a category 'popular art,'" he made quotation marks on the air, "but it's something wholly other, and yes I'd say less, than art."

Hugh put his head down on his arm as though to weep. "Okay, cracker, you're telling me Jimi Hendrix is a 'mere'"—he made histrionic quotation marks on the air around the word he sneered as much as said—"popular artist, and we'll forget the fact that every motherfucker in the past who's now high art was in his own time pop art, but I'm wondering if you're putting Ella Fitzgerald, Louis Armstrong, and Duke Ellington in that ghetto. I'm wondering also if that ghetto is mixed, if you've got Charlie Chaplin in there or Mark Twain."

"Your point is well taken, except that Jazz has always had a tenuous relation to the marketplace, and that in the case of someone like Charley Chaplin, or Louis Armstrong for that matter, the truly original practitioners of a popular art form are transcendent. They achieve something akin to high art by virtue of their originality," Ned asserted. "So, yeah, there are exceptions, and I suppose the question is whether Hendrix was original in the sense that, to the extent that, say, Armstrong or Billie Holiday were original."

"Goddamned white people," Hugh chuckled and blithely performed with his partner Ned whatever fancy soul handshake was in fashion. He smiled and dipped his chin to me as he trotted off to hear about isomers.

"Was that for real?" I asked Ned, and suddenly wished I hadn't.

But he took it in the correct spirit. "Just sparring, man. I don't know shit about art. Not really. We just like to mess around like that," he said.

"So you don't believe there's real art and, like, popular art," I said as a statement rather than a question, trying to get something started back up.

"Yeah, sure, I believe. And I believe to call anything art, pop or serious or up your bung with a rubber hose, is like believing the sign of the beast is six six six and some youngin in Bumfuck's got it right under his hairline. Art's a matter of faith just like all that other mumbo jumbo, just like religion." Ned was a smart guy.

"But wait a minute," I protested. "What isn't a matter of faith, then? And just what the fuck's faith? I mean, it seems a lot easier to believe something's art than it is to believe a priest can go abracadabra and turn wine into Holy Blood."

"It might be easier for you, little bro, but to me they're the same thing. To a lot of people, especially a lot of artists, it ain't easy believing in art, believing that it's special the way most people assume it is. But dig, assuming something's not the same thing as having faith. Idiots and children assume. You're not thinking until you're no longer taking anything for granted. Figure out what you're taking for granted, then scare the shit out of yourself by looking at it real hard until it starts seeming weird. Music? Noise? What's the diff, really? Love? Chemicals and fairytales. Art? Various structures we're conditioned to respond to with a range of behaviors, all anchored to ye ol' Pleasure Principle: eating, drinking and screwing."

I wanted to occupy a world of smart talk and big ideas; I wanted to join the exclusive club of world-weary cynics. I wanted to condescend, credibly, to all whose horizons extended no farther than the chimeras of the marketplace. I was nineteen, living with a suicidal older woman, attending a community college at the end of a war that destroyed America's spirit, or destroyed one and infused it with yet another whose character, like my own, was grounded in narcissism, a self-gazing wonder that verged on the holy.

As I blinked in the sun, I thought of the kata I was composing: for several weeks I'd been making up a karate dance, something I'd never thought to do before. The kata, I was pretty sure, were ancient; performing them, one touched upon something old and good, something tested. In Sasebo, Japan, my sensei, a famous ninth-degree black belt in his late sixties named Yasozato-san, had subcontracted, so to speak, the teaching of the more advanced kata to Takafugi-san, a blithe, stern acolyte and fifth-degree black belt who spoke not a word of English, but seemed to understand it better than Sensei. He drilled me maniacally, until the dances were carved into my life, and I simply couldn't conceive of moving in any patterns but those; however, days earlier, with no forethought or contemplation, I'd begun composing a dance, one constructed of pieces of all the kata I knew but in combinations wholly different from anything Takafugi had carved into me. It was a kind of sorrow dance, but I didn't know it at the time; I danced my sorrow and was exhilarated to do so. In the dance, I was attacked by five men, all of them my criminal father, my poor, sick, ruined father; I stood between them and the ghost of my mother, a ghost I couldn't see or hear. I protected the ghost of my mother from my fragmented father, and I was transported by the dance to the fount of all sorrow, and it poured over me, anointed me. It was thus I healed myself, a little.

As I blinked back the early-afternoon sun, emerging from the cave that was the cafeteria, I saw, across the commons, Cameron talking to his mother. They just stood and chatted, smiling, sometimes laughing; he shielded his eyes from the sun. She angled into a shadow. They looked so much alike they must have seen themselves in each other. I tried to see their auras, see the colors around their bodies, but that was futile because I assumed that the whole notion of auras was false, so I stood a long minute trying to shatter that assumption. Larry Schwartz, one of the renegade history instructors, joined Cameron and his mother, and they stood smiling and conversing, laughing every few moments. They were contented, happy in one another's company. Schwartz walked away laughing and waving and mother and son remained in one another's happy regard, at peace with the mysteries of life, in the midst of a friendship that seemed, for its uncluttered ease and casual grace, in the bright aura of that day, a kind of miracle.